Christian Jr./Sr High School
2100 Greenfield Dr.
El Cajon, CA 92019

1st EDITION

Perspectives on Modern World History

Stalin's Great Purge

1st EDITION

Perspectives on Modern World History

Stalin's Great Purge

Noah Berlatsky

Editor

GREENHAVEN PRESS
A part of Gale, Cengage Learning

GALE
CENGAGE Learning

Detroit • New York • San Francisco • New Haven, Conn • Waterville, Maine • London

Elizabeth Des Chenes, *Director, Publishing Solutions*

© 2013 Greenhaven Press, a part of Gale, Cengage Learning.

Gale and Greenhaven Press are registered trademarks used herein under license.

For more information, contact:
Greenhaven Press
27500 Drake Rd.
Farmington Hills, MI 48331-3535
Or you can visit our Internet site at gale.cengage.com.

For product information and technology assistance, contact us at
Gale Customer Support, 1-800-877-4253.

For permission to use material from this text or product, submit all requests online at
www.cengage.com/permissions.

Further permissions questions can be e-mailed to permissionrequest@cengage.com.

Articles in Greenhaven Press anthologies are often edited for length to meet page requirements. In addition, original titles of these works are changed to clearly present the main thesis and to explicitly indicate the author's opinion. Every effort is made to ensure that Greenhaven Press accurately reflects the original intent of the authors. Every effort has been made to trace the owners of copyrighted material.

Cover image © Hulton-Deutsch Collection/Corbis and © Hulton Archive/Getty Images.

LIBRARY OF CONGRESS CATALOGING-IN-PUBLICATION DATA

Stalin's great purge / Noah Berlatsky, book editor.
   p. cm. -- (Perspectives on modern world history)
   Includes bibliographical references and index.
   ISBN 978-0-7377-6371-3 (hardcover)
  1. Political purges--Soviet Union--History. 2. Political purges--Soviet Union--History--Sources. 3. Stalin, Joseph, 1879–1953. 4. Kommunisticheskaia partiia Sovetskogo Soiuza--Purges. 5. Soviet Union--Politics and government--1936–1953. 6. Soviet Union--Politics and government--1936–1953 --Sources. 7. Soviet Union--Social conditions. 8. Soviet Union--Social conditions--Sources. I. Berlatsky, Noah.
   DK268.4.S728 2012
   947.084'2--dc23
                                      2012016630

Printed in the United States of America
1 2 3 4 5 6 7 16 15 14 13 12

CONTENTS

CHAPTER 3   Personal Narratives

FOREWORD

"History cannot give us a program for the future, but it can give us a fuller understanding of ourselves, and of our common humanity, so that we can better face the future."

—Robert Penn Warren,
American poet and novelist

The history of each nation is punctuated by momentous events that represent turning points for that nation, with an impact felt far beyond its borders. These events—displaying the full range of human capabilities, from violence, greed, and ignorance to heroism, courage, and strength—are nearly always complicated and multifaceted. Any student of history faces the challenge of grasping the many strands that constitute such world-changing events as wars, social movements, and environmental disasters. But understanding these significant historic events can be enhanced by exposure to a variety of perspectives, whether of people involved intimately or of ones observing from a distance of miles or years. Understanding can also be increased by learning about the controversies surrounding such events and exploring hot-button issues from multiple angles. Finally, true understanding of important historic events involves knowledge of the events' human impact—of the ways such events affected people in their everyday lives—all over the world.

Perspectives on Modern World History examines global historic events from the twentieth century onward by presenting analysis and observation from numerous vantage points. Each volume offers high school, early college level, and general interest readers a thematically arranged anthology of previously published materials that address a major historical event, with an emphasis on international coverage. Each volume opens with background information on the event, then presents the controversies surrounding that event, and concludes with first-person narratives from people who lived through the event or were affected by it. By providing primary sources from the time of the event, as well as relevant commentary surrounding the event, this series can be used to inform debate, help develop critical thinking skills, increase global awareness, and enhance an understanding of international perspectives on history.

Material in each volume is selected from a diverse range of sources, including journals, magazines, newspapers, nonfiction books, personal narratives, speeches, congressional testimony, government documents, pamphlets, organization newsletters, and position papers. Articles taken from these sources are carefully edited and introduced to provide context and background. Each volume of Perspectives on Modern World History includes an array of views on events of global significance. Much of the material comes from international sources and from US sources that provide extensive international coverage.

Each volume in the Perspectives on Modern World History series also includes:

- A full-color **world map**, offering context and geographic perspective.
- An annotated **table of contents** that provides a brief summary of each essay in the volume.
- An **introduction** specific to the volume topic.
- For each viewpoint, a brief **introduction** that has notes about the author and source of the viewpoint, and that provides a summary of its main points.
- Full-color **charts**, **graphs**, **maps**, and other visual representations.

- Informational **sidebars** that explore the lives of key individuals, give background on historical events, or explain scientific or technical concepts.
- A **glossary** that defines key terms, as needed.
- A **chronology** of important dates preceding, during, and immediately following the event.
- A **bibliography** of additional books, periodicals, and websites for further research.
- A comprehensive **subject index** that offers access to people, places, and events cited in the text.

Perspectives on Modern World History is designed for a broad spectrum of readers who want to learn more about not only history but also current events, political science, government, international relations, and sociology—students doing research for class assignments or debates, teachers and faculty seeking to supplement course materials, and others wanting to improve their understanding of history. Each volume of Perspectives on Modern World History is designed to illuminate a complicated event, to spark debate, and to show the human perspective behind the world's most significant happenings of recent decades.

INTRODUCTION

Today Joseph Stalin is known in the West as one of history's most vicious tyrants and mass murderers. But while he was in power, there were many in the West who supported his regime. British playwright George Bernard Shaw, for example, defended Stalin's show trials of old revolutionary leaders, saying that sometimes such people "had to be pushed off the ladder with a rope around their necks." The great Chilean poet Pablo Neruda also admired Stalin. So did the French philosopher and writer Jean-Paul Sartre. *New York Times* reporter Walter Duranty described Stalin as "the greatest living statesman." Duranty denied reports of the terrifying famine in Ukraine, where millions were being deliberately starved to death by Stalin's policies. Instead, Duranty insisted that when he had traveled in the region, the people were "healthier and more cheerful" than he had expected. Many others—from Communist rebels fighting against the fascist regime in 1930s Spain to Communist and leftist groups in Britain, France, and the United States—saw Stalin as a hero and the Soviet Union as a potential utopia.

How was it possible that so many people supported such a horrific ruler? Commentators suggest different answers. Some conservative writers have argued that there is continuity between liberalism and Stalinism. They say that leftists approved of Stalin because leftist ideology naturally leads to Stalinism. For instance, James Lewis, in an August 12, 2009, article in the *American Thinker*, argues that US president Barack Obama had many associates on the radical Left who believed that their enemies were evil and had to be destroyed. Lewis argues, "Stalin is dead. But Stalinism lives because that kind of cold, calculating, and destructive 'idealism' seems to appeal to certain personalities."

Similarly, Bruce S. Thornton in a June 16, 2009, essay in *City Journal* argues that "The long romance of Western leftists with some of the bloodiest regimes and political movements in history is a story not told often enough." He says that the attraction of leftists to Stalin connects with what he sees as their attraction to other vicious Communist regimes, such as that of Mao Tse-tung in China. He also argues that it is consistent with what he argues is leftist defenses of radical Islam. Thornton concludes that leftists have consistently attacked the "institutions and ideals" that make freedom, democracy, and affluence possible. He says that part of this attack is "extolling enemies who seek to destroy all of these goods." Thus, for Thornton, leftist support for Stalin is consistent with what he sees as a general leftist attack on humanity and decency.

Other commentators reject the view that there is something intrinsic to liberal or radical views, which made Stalin appealing. Instead, many critics say that leftists were fooled by Stalin's claims to be creating an equal and just society. Australian economist John Quiggin, for example, says that those who supported Stalin, "may fairly be accused of gullibility and wishful thinking in their assessment of the Soviet Union, but this does not imply that their own ideas contained the seeds of totalitarianism." Brian Landers, in *American and Russian Imperialism*, agrees, arguing that Stalin appealed to "thousands of men and women . . . who needed to believe that the inhumanities, inequalities, and exploitation that they saw in their own societies could be abolished."

Some support for Stalin outside the Soviet Union was helped along by practical considerations. For example, during the Spanish Civil War, rebels fighting against the authoritarian fascist regime of Francisco Franco turned to Stalin's regime for help. "What wonder if [the anti-Franco forces] saw in Stalin the saviour of the anti-fascist war?," US Communist activist and anti-Stalinist Emma Goldman said.

Similarly, Winston Churchill, prime minister of Great Britain during World War II, badly needed the aid of the Soviet Union in the fight against Nazi Germany. Perhaps in part for that reason, Churchill came to see Stalin as a reasonable man and a worthy ally. In 1945, Stalin had already murdered millions of people and launched particularly vicious terror campaigns in Poland. Yet Churchill wrote privately, "Stalin I'm sure means well to the world and Poland."

If Churchill's wishful thinking about Stalin was naive, the attitude of the US administration was no wiser. US ambassador to Russia Joseph Davies seemed determined to ignore any evidence of Stalin's misdeeds. According to an article by Ronald Radosh in the *National Review*, "When Davies's wife, Marjorie Merriweather Post, was woken up at night by gun blasts across the street as NKVD [Soviet secret police] agents murdered prisoners, her husband would explain that she was hearing the sound of drilling for Stalin's new Moscow metro." Davies also attended Stalin's show trials of political opponents in 1936 and insisted that the accused were guilty as charged and that the confessions, obtained under torture, were genuine. Davies' reports were welcomed in Washington, where President Franklin Roosevelt was working to form an alliance with the Soviet Union against the growing danger of Nazi Germany.

Not everyone at the time was fooled by Stalin. William Bullitt, the US ambassador to Russia before Davies, justly accused Stalin of "mass murder." US anarchist and Communist activist Emma Goldman denounced Stalin repeatedly. In 1935 she wrote:

There is more governmental terrorism in Soviet Russia than anywhere else in the civilized world today, for

Stalin has to conquer and enslave a stubborn peasantry of a hundred millions. It is popular hatred of the regime which explains the stupendous industrial sabotage in Russia, the disorganization of the transport after sixteen years of virtual military management; the terrific famine in the South and Southeast, notwithstanding favorable natural conditions and in spite of the severest measures to compel the peasants to sow and reap, in spite even of wholesale extermination and of the deportation of more than a million peasants to forced labor camps.

In 1956, Nikita Khrushchev, Stalin's successor, delivered a speech in which he denounced Stalin, accusing him of unjustly murdering and imprisoning his opponents. With Stalin's crimes exposed, many of those who had praised him rethought their positions. The Communist Party in the United States, which had already dwindled, lost thousands more members. Many who had vocally supported Stalin, such as folk singer Pete Seeger, repudiated him (Seeger said he thought Stalin had been a "hard driver" and found instead that he was a "cruel deceiver"). Some who had supported communism moved to more conservative beliefs. Others, according to John Quiggin, "simply accepted they had made a mistaken judgment, and adopted a more skeptical view of life, while retaining their old ideals."

Today there are some in Russia who admire Stalin for making Russia strong and for achieving victory in World War II. There are even some in the West who still support Stalin; the Stalin Society in Great Britain meets regularly to discuss and admire his legacy. However, the Stalin Society's membership is small and largely "elderly to the point of decrepitude," according to Johann Hari in a June 10, 2002, article in the *New Statesman.* For the most part in the West, Stalin has joined Hitler as a figure that very few praise or seek to emulate.

In *Perspectives on Modern World History: Stalin's Great Purge* authors offer varying analyses of the atrocities that occurred under Stalin's reign in the Soviet Union and his regime's lasting impact on the world today.

World Map

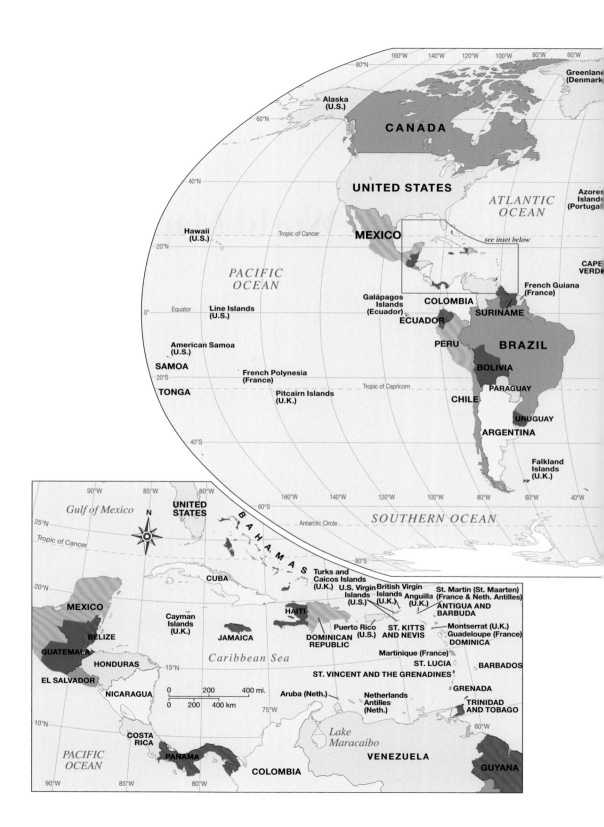

Alaska
(U.S.)

CANADA

UNITED STATES

ATLANTIC
OCEAN

Azores
Islands
(Portugal)

Hawaii
(U.S.)

Tropic of Cancer

MEXICO

see inset below

CAPE
VERDE

PACIFIC
OCEAN

Galápagos
Islands
(Ecuador)

COLOMBIA

French Guiana
(France)

Line Islands
(U.S.)

Equator

ECUADOR

SURINAME

American Samoa
(U.S.)

PERU

BRAZIL

SAMOA

Tropic of Capricorn

BOLIVIA

TONGA

French Polynesia
(France)

PARAGUAY

Pitcairn Islands
(U.K.)

CHILE

URUGUAY

ARGENTINA

Falkland
Islands
(U.K.)

SOUTHERN OCEAN

Antarctic Circle

Greenland
(Denmark)

Gulf of Mexico

UNITED
STATES

N

BAHAMAS

Tropic of Cancer

Turks and
Caicos Islands
(U.K.)

U.S. Virgin
Islands
(U.S.)

British Virgin
Islands
(U.K.)

St. Martin (St. Maarten)
(France & Neth. Antilles)

MEXICO

CUBA

Anguilla
(U.K.)

ANTIGUA AND
BARBUDA

Cayman
Islands
(U.K.)

HAITI

BELIZE

JAMAICA

Puerto Rico
(U.S.)

DOMINICAN
REPUBLIC

ST. KITTS
AND NEVIS

Montserrat (U.K.)
Guadeloupe (France)
DOMINICA

GUATEMALA

Caribbean Sea

Martinique (France)

ST. LUCIA

BARBADOS

HONDURAS

EL SALVADOR

ST. VINCENT AND THE GRENADINES

NICARAGUA

0   200   400 mi.

0   200   400 km

Aruba (Neth.)

Netherlands
Antilles
(Neth.)

GRENADA

TRINIDAD
AND TOBAGO

COSTA
RICA

PACIFIC
OCEAN

PANAMA

COLOMBIA

Lake
Maracaibo

VENEZUELA

GUYANA

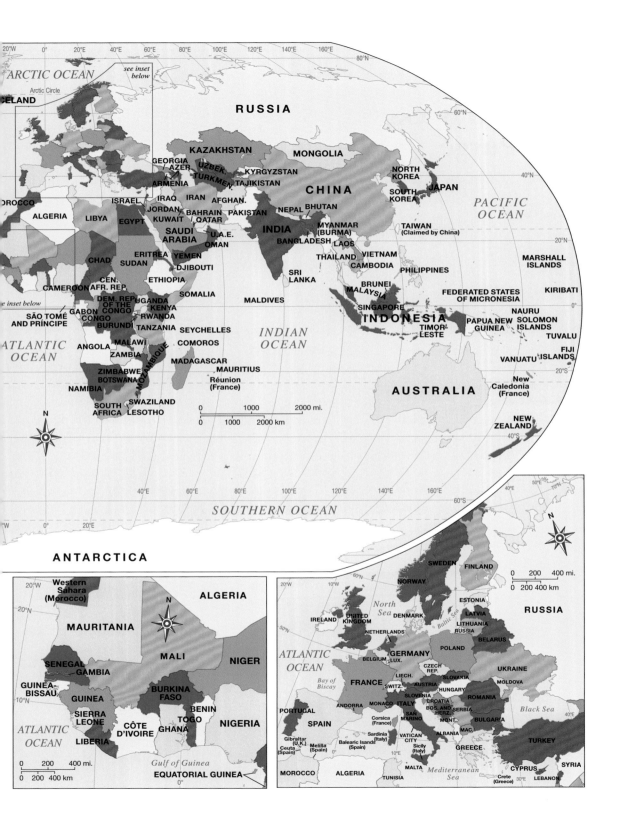

CHAPTER 1

Historical Background on Stalin's Great Purge

Overview of the Great Purge

Hiroaki Kuromiya

In the following viewpoint, a historian explains that there were two kinds of purges in Russia. The first kind, he says, was the expulsion of political opponents from the Communist Party. The second kind of purge, he argues, was a deliberate weapon of political terror, used to murder and imprison vast numbers of opponents and imagined opponents. This form of terror was used throughout the Communist reign but reached its height under Joseph Stalin, particularly from 1935 to 1938. Stalin, the author argues, used the purges to enforce obedience in the face of unpopular policies such as the collectivization of agriculture, which resulted in massive famine in Ukraine and elsewhere. Purges continued into the 1950s, he says, though with much less ferocity and loss of life. Hiroaki Kuromiya is a professor of history at Indiana University and the author of *Stalin*.

Photo on previous page: A statue in honor of Joseph Stalin stands in the main square of Gori, Georgia, his birthplace. Although still revered by some, the Russian leader is generally believed to have been a brutal dictator. (© **Cliff Volpe/ Getty Images**.)

SOURCE. Hiroaki Kuromiya, *Europe Since 1914: Encyclopedia of the Age of War and Reconstruction*, ed. John Merriman and Jay Winter. Belmont, CA: Charles Scribner's Sons, 2006, pp. 2131–2136. EUR 1914–2002 5V SET. © 2006 Gale, a part of Cengage Learning, Inc. Reproduced by permission. www.cengage.com/permissions.

The term *purge* has a peculiarly ominous tone because it has been intimately associated with the terror in communist countries. In fact, historically it denotes two distinct political operations in the Soviet Union. One was a process whereby institutions such as the state bureaucracies and the Communist Party sought to expel (purge) those functionaries suspected of political deviation and professional incompetence: leftovers from the old regime, former members of non-Bolshevik[1] political parties, political oppositionists, and others deemed politically unreliable or professionally incompetent. The other was political repression and terror, a purge of society in general from "enemies."

Purge as Routine Cleansing

The first process was not necessarily free from terror, but it was not meant to be a terror operation. It was most famously associated with the repeated "cleansing" operations within the Communist Party. Not dissimilar in kind from the exclusion of Nazi members from state institutions in postwar Germany or, in postcommunist Eastern Europe, of those associated with the secret police and political terror, the cleansings were meant to keep the party free from opportunists and other undesirable elements. Two specific factors made purges of the party inevitable. One is that whereas the party needed a broad mass political base and wished to broaden its membership, as it did first in 1917 when the party emerged from underground and expanded rapidly, it also had to maintain its political purity as a communist avant-garde party. The other is that the absence of pluralism and the system of one-party dictatorship necessitated purges. Since those who sought political activity, even those who disagreed with the Communist Party, had nowhere else to go and therefore sought to channel the Communist Party from within in the direction they desired, the party appeared constantly diluted by subversives who had to be removed. Scholars of "totalitarianism" have developed an elaborate theory on the need for a "permanent purge" for maintaining the party's revolutionary élan [zeal] by eliminating the corrupt and the deviant.

The constant purge process did not appear adequate to the party leaders when they decided on sudden and radical policy changes. Therefore the Communist Party resorted periodically to party-wide purge campaigns. Some early cases had already occurred in 1918–1919 when the party was deeply involved in the civil war against the counterrevolutionaries.[2] The first major party-wide purge campaign took place in 1921–1922, when the party was forced by economic necessity to retreat from revolutionary war to peaceful economic reconstruction (the New Economic Policy or NEP) through a partial reintroduction of market relations. This purge reduced the membership by nearly a quarter. The purge was followed by a rapid expansion of party ranks in the mid-1920s, particularly after the death of Vladimir Lenin, the leader of the party, through special recruitment campaigns of workers. Toward the end of the 1920s Joseph Stalin emerged as the victor in the struggle for power among the party elite and, ending NEP, turned to enact his "revolution from above" (rapid industrialization and wholesale collectivization [of farms]). This inaugurated another party-wide purge carried out purportedly to strengthen the party's "fighting capacity." This purge was enacted simultaneously with recruitment campaigns to further "proletarianize." Yet by 1933, when Stalin's "revolution from above" had confronted a grave crisis owing to widespread famine, recruitment was terminated and another party-wide purge was executed. The party leadership found that many formerly trustworthy functionaries were not in sympathy with the harsh economic and political measures taken to cope with the famine crisis. As a result, a very large number of party members fell victim to the purge. The 1933 purge still failed to satisfy the party leaders, who continued membership inspection in various forms for the next several years. This process merged with the second kind of purge, terror and repression, in the mid- to late 1930s against the backdrop of the increasing threat of war [World War II]. From 1933 to 1938 the Communist Party membership thus declined by more than 40 percent, from 3.5 million to 1.9 million.

> The purge of the 1930s created . . . problems, starting with the chaos of bookkeeping and ending with the destruction of the lives of numerous loyal party members.

The purge of the 1930s created a host of problems, starting with the chaos of bookkeeping and ending with the destruction of the lives of numerous loyal party members. So traumatic was the experience that Stalin, addressing the Eighteenth Party Congress in 1939, declared that although the purge campaign strengthened the party by expelling the politically unreliable, grave mistakes had been committed during the campaigns and that the party would have no need to resort to further mass cleansings. Indeed, such mass operations were officially abolished and were never to be repeated.

This did not mean that routine purges disappeared. They continued. Moreover, localized purges also took place in various areas of the country, for example, in those areas of the Soviet Union occupied during World War II (including the newly incorporated union republics such as the Baltic states), in order to purge the party of those members suspected of desertion, collaboration with enemy forces, and other crimes.

Purge as Terror

Purge as political terror began immediately after the October Revolution [the Russian Revolution of 1917]. The new revolutionary government created a secret police (Cheka) soon after the revolution to fight the counter-

A Novelist Who Experienced the Purges Re-creates the Terror of the Time

It was cold, dark and very quiet on the staircase. The younger of the two men from the Commissariat of the Interior proposed to shoot the lock of the door to pieces. Vassilij leant against the lift door; he had not had the time to put on his boots properly, and his hands trembled so much that he could not tie the laces. The elder of the two men was against shooting; the arrest had to be carried out discreetly. They both blew on their stiff hands and began again to hammer against the door; the younger banged on it with the butt of his revolver. A few floors below them a woman screamed in a piercing voice. "Tell her to shut up," said the young man to Vassilij. "Be quiet," shouted Vassilij. "Here is Authority." The woman became quiet at once. The young man changed over to belabouring the door with his boots. The noise filled the whole staircase; at last the door fell open.

The three of them stood by Rubashov's bed, the young man with his pistol in his hand, the old man holding himself stiffly as though standing to attention; Vassilij stood a few steps behind them, leaning against the wall. Rubashov was still drying the sweat from the back of his head; he looked at them shortsightedly with sleepy eyes. "Citizen Rubashov, Nicholas Salmanovitch, we arrest you in the name of the law," said the young man.

SOURCE: Arthur Koestler, Darkness at Noon: A Novel. New York: Scribner, 1941, pp. 6–7.

revolutionary forces. During the civil war that followed (1918–1921), as many as 150,000 death sentences were given in the country. Even this figure is probably underestimated. During the relatively peaceful NEP (1921–1927), approximately 10,000 people ("political criminals") were sentenced to death by the secret police (from 1923, the OGPU). Stalin's "revolution from above," which marked a sharp turn from NEP and met resistance both from within the party and the government and from Soviet society in general, led to a sharp increase in the number of political death sentences meted out. In the four years from 1928 to 1931 more than 30,000 were sentenced to death in the country for political crimes. . . .

> This new, class-neutral image of enemy encompassed virtually anyone, including tried and tested party members.

These numbers are merely the tip of the iceberg. During the four years of Stalin's "revolution from above" almost half a million people were arrested for alleged political and economic crimes (such as "economic wrecking"), most of whom were sentenced to prison terms or exile. It was at this time that the infamous gulag (soviet labor camps) expanded rapidly. In collectivizing the countryside, the party purged it of the kulaks (rich peasants), branded as "class enemies" (rural bourgeois), and their supporters. This dekulakization operation dispossessed probably more than three million peasants. In addition, in 1928–1932 more than ten million people fled the countryside to the city, a large number of whom did so involuntarily.

When the immediate goals of Stalin's "revolution from above" were achieved, the purge operation declined to a degree, as far as the number of death sentences were concerned—about seven thousand much lower than the previous few years. The number of arrests remained very high, however, amounting to close to half a million. This reflected the fact that Stalin used political purges as terror widely during the famine of 1932–1933 (which itself claimed several million lives). The famine crisis and the terror used to cope with it marked a new stage in the history of Soviet purge. Up until then, the main target of the purge was the "class enemy," but during the famine crisis the target began to shift subtly from the "class enemy" to the "enemy of the people." This new, class-neutral image of enemy encompassed virtually anyone, including tried and tested party members. The famous Soviet prosecutor Andrei Vyshinsky under Stalin noted in 1933 that having lost the battle, the enemy now resorted to "methods known as quiet sapping" rather than direct frontal attack and sought to conceal its wrecking acts with all sorts of "objective reasons," "defects," and the contention that the incidents did "not seem to be caused by malicious human intent." Therefore, Vyshinsky emphasized, the enemy "becomes less detectable and hence it becomes less possible to isolate him."

This meant that mass purges were inevitable in order to capture hidden enemies, even at the cost of the innocent. Indeed, it was then, 1932–1934, that even Communist Party members began to be arrested in great numbers and even executed as enemies. It was then that, against the background of international threat from the east (Japan) and the west (Germany), foreigners, foreign-born Soviet citizens, and those associated with them came under suspicion and were purged in significant numbers. Thus, many individuals born in Harbin [China], Warsaw [Poland], Riga [Latvia], Bucharest [Hungary], and elsewhere were purged (executed) for their alleged foreign connections. Even party members who hailed from abroad (Koreans, Bulgarians, Poles, Ukrainians, Russians, and others) were subjected to the same fate. Numerous people (Poles, Ukrainians, and others) were arrested and executed for their alleged membership in "nationalist" organizations or in foreign (German, Japanese, Polish) "spy networks" (almost all of these accusations were fabricated by the secret police). The government began to collect data on all "suspect" national groups (such as ethnic Germans) in the country. All this paled, however, in comparison with what came to be known as the Great Purge (or Great Terror).

The Great Purges

There is no universally accepted consensus on exactly when Stalin started the Great Purge. Many concerned with Ukraine, which was hard hit by the famine and the

Women harvest hay in 1941 outside Moscow. Farm collectives like this one were a crucial part of Stalin's socialist plans for the Soviet Union. (© Margaret Bourke-White/Time & Life Pictures/Getty Images.)

purge in 1932–1933, contend that it began at that time. Some assert that it began with the murder of Sergei Kirov, the head of the Leningrad party organization, in December 1934. Some suggest that Stalin launched it with the first Moscow show trial in August 1936. Yet others attribute it to the summer of 1937 when indisputably mass terror operations began. Most scholars tend to agree, however, that the Great Purge virtually came to a halt by the autumn of 1938, when Stalin's chief executioner, the secret police chief Nikolai Yezhov, was removed from his post. In the four years from 1935 through 1938, nearly 2 million (in 1937 and 1938 alone more than 1.3 million) people were arrested. Of them, nearly 700,000 were sentenced to death. Although these data are almost certainly incomplete, the two years of 1937 and 1938 account for 99 percent of these death sentences. The execution rate of the arrested was 44 percent in 1937 and 59 percent in 1938, whereas it was less than 1 percent in 1935 and 1936.

Who was purged? It used to be believed that the main victims of the purge were the Soviet elite. Most famously, the three Moscow show trials (held in 1936, 1937, and 1938) highlighted prominent Bolsheviks (such as Grigory Zinoviev, Lev Kamenev, Georgy Pyatakov, and Nikolai Bukharin), most of whom were executed immediately after their trials. While it is likely that the elite suffered disproportionately because of their visibility and their positions of responsibility, in fact "little people"— workers, peasants, and other "ordinary" Soviet citizens—accounted numerically for the majority of the victims, as became clear after the opening up of previously closed Soviet archives in the 1990s.[3] Formerly repressed kulaks, criminals, ministers of religion, and other politically "undesirable" elements were specifically targeted by a special mass operation in 1937–1938 (the so-called kulak operation). Many others, such as the unemployed and the elderly, regarded as socially "unproductive" and dependent were purged along with other target groups. In some cases, even those already incarcerated were executed as if imprisonment were not enough. Similarly, specific national groups (particularly "diaspora nations" in the Soviet Union such as ethnic Germans, Poles, Greeks, Latvians, Koreans, and Chinese) were targeted for purge in special mass operations ("national operations") in 1937–1938. Many people who were associated in one way or another with those targeted groups of people were also purged. Although these mass operations initially had concrete numerical goals for arrest and execution, in the course of their implementation a competition-like frenzy by the

> "The unemployed and the elderly, regarded as socially 'unproductive' and dependent were purged along with other target groups."

secret police operatives, which in turn was sanctioned by Stalin, resulted in numbers that far exceeded the original goals. . . .

Theories of the Purges

The vast majority of those purged in these years (and, for that matter, before and after under Stalin) have been rehabilitated since as innocent victims of Stalin's terror. Why did the Great Purge take place at all? There is much scholarly debate on this and there is no consensus. Some influential older theories, which explain certain aspects of the Great Purge well, have proved inadequate to explain its extent: that Stalin wanted to remove all former oppositionists, particularly the old Bolsheviks who possessed a degree of independence of mind, or that Stalin wanted to replace old elite cadres with young ones. One new theory is that the Great Purge was part of a gigantic social engineering attempt. However, this fails to explain the concentration of the killings in just two years (1937 and 1938) and the necessity of killing rather than incarceration, let alone the implementation of the "national operations." Another theory is that Stalin indeed faced a growing internal threat in the country, especially from the "dekulakized" peasants and other repressed elements.

> Stalin and his henchmen . . . never failed to defend the Great Purge as an absolute necessity.

Yet this interpretation has so far not shown whether the threat indeed existed or whether the threat had increased so much that Stalin suddenly felt compelled to initiate mass purge operations. Yet another theory, which is not entirely new, claims that it was a preemptive strike against all real and imagined enemies who might pose a grave political threat from within in case of war from without. This, according to critics, fails to explain the social engineering aspects of the purge. So the debate continues.

It is noteworthy that Stalin and his henchmen such as Vyacheslav Molotov and Lazar Kaganovich never failed to defend the Great Purge as an absolute necessity even though some mistakes were made and innocent people suffered. Their justification was that without the Great Purge the country would have lost to Nazi Germany because the internal "enemies of the people" would have risen up against the Soviet government. It was the Great Purge that made it possible to secure the rear for war. Such a justification has been equally passionately disputed by many who claim that the country won the war against Nazi Germany not thanks to the Great Purges or Stalin's leadership but in spite of the Purge and in spite of Stalin.

How Soviet society reacted to the Great Purge is another difficult issue. Some appeared to support the terror against the "enemies of the people" without question, while others merely toed the official line. Many upwardly mobile individuals benefited from the purges, but there were also people who did question what appeared to be madness. Still, there were very, very few cases of open dissent, because even those Soviet citizens who did not believe in the actions of the government were intimidated or frightened and generally could not, or did not, try to understand what was happening.

After the Great Purge

Purges did not cease with the end of the Great Purge. At reduced levels, they continued. The areas newly incorporated into the Soviet Union in 1939–1940 were thoroughly purged of "bourgeois" and other suspect elements. The war against Nazi Germany intensified the hunt for suspected spies, defeatists, deserters, and others, and after the war many people suspected of collaboration were purged. During and after the war Stalin questioned the political loyalty of certain ethnic groups (Chechens, Crimean Tatars, and others) and resorted to brutal ethnic cleansings by removing them entirely from their native lands. All the Soviet POWs and civilian laborers repatriated from Germany after the war were carefully screened and many were purged. In western borderlands such as western Ukraine, where nationalist forces continued to fight a civil war against the Soviet forces into the 1950s, the purge operations were extraordinarily brutal. However, the Great Purge was not repeated. Even most of those Soviet citizens who took arms against the Red Army managed to survive in the gulag. Thus it was in 1950 that the gulag population reached its peak under Stalin.

> The purges terrorized the entire country, both the elite and the ordinary people.

In sum, whereas the purges devastated the entire nation, they served the political leadership well by removing suspect members from the Communist Party, the government, and Soviet society in general. The necessity for purges, which were conducted routinely and sometimes violently, stemmed in large part from the system of one-party dictatorship and the lack of political pluralism. Stalin's obsession with "enemies" made the purges an integral part of Soviet politics. The purges terrorized the entire country, both the elite and the ordinary people, affecting, in one way or another, nearly every family in the Soviet Union under Stalin. Although the purges were not necessarily unpopular, the majority of the population had no choice but to accept them and live on the terms dictated by the regime.

Notes

1. The Bolsheviks were the Communist Party faction founded by Vladimir Lenin that took power in Russia.
2. The Communist Party took power in 1917. A civil war followed, in which the United States and many other nations sent troops to fight the Communists.
3. The Soviet Union collapsed in 1991.

Stalin's Five-Year Plan Created Hardship

Gareth Jones

In the following viewpoint, a Welsh journalist reports that agriculture failed in Russia under Stalin's economic plan. He says that one reason for this was that wealthy peasants, or kulaks, resisted the collectivization of agriculture, in which individual privately-owned farms were collected into large state-owned farms. Rather than give up their livestock to the government, he says, some kulaks slaughtered their animals. Many kulaks were also exiled, and so could not work the land. He says poor transportation also interfered with the distribution of crops. The author concludes that crop yields were far lower than expected, and Russia faced serious famine. Gareth Jones was a Welsh journalist who publicized the Ukrainian famine during the 1930s.

I n my first article on present-day conditions in Russia in Saturday's [April 4, 1931] *Western Mail,* I referred to the failure of crops under the Five-Year Plan.

SOURCE. Gareth Jones, "'Will There Be Soup?' Russia Famished Under the Five-Year Plan," *Western Mail,* April 11, 1931. Copyright © 1931 by MediaWales. All rights reserved. Reproduced by permission.

Counter Revolution

One reason why the harvest of all crops, vegetables as well as grain have failed is that a couple of million of the most energetic *kulaks* (the richest peasants) have been exiled. An account of this I heard in the morning after a night on the wooden floor of the stuffy room which I shared with the whole of the peasant's family.

I walked along to see the Communist president of the village Soviet, a sharp, square jawed young man in a green military cap.

"Jump into my carriage," he said and in a few minutes we were bumping over the fields of the collective farm.

"We have had a great victory here," he said as we looked back on the several hundred huts in the village. "We've defeated the *kulaks,* those peasants who had a lot of land and employed labour. We exiled 14 families from here and now they're cutting wood in the forests of the north or working in Siberia [the vast, frigid north-eastern part of Russia]. We must root them out because they are of the enemy class. We sent the last *kulak* a month ago."

"What had he done?" I asked.

He was very religious and had a sect of his own. He used to collect the peasants in his hut and tell them that the Communist wanted the peasants to starve but that there would be a war and when there was war the Pope of Rome would come to their village and hang all the Communists. That was counter-revolution. So we send him away. These *kulaks* are terrible. It was they that urged the peasants to massacre their cattle.

And he told me how killing the cattle and horses throughout Russia was another reason why food was scarce. [Joseph] Stalin in his speech in June 1930 estimated that one-third of the cattle and at least 1/5 of the horses of Russia had been massacred by peasants who did not wish to give up the animals for nothing to collective [state-run] farms.

Gloomy Forecast

Some days after my conversations in this village I was seated in a slowly moving train which six days before had left Tashkent in Central Asia and was now carrying me from Samara to Moscow.

I glanced out of the window and suddenly saw a mass of debris-shattered coaches [and] torn up rails. There had been an accident and a goods train had obviously rattled down a slope. It gave me another clue as to why food was so short, and that is bad transport.

Under the Five-Year Plan [a government plan for economic growth and industrialization] courageous efforts . . . [have] been made to improve the railway system. Miles of new railroads have been laid, numbers of new Soviet locomotives have been built, yet the railways are

In 1932 Russia, a group of peasant women share the little food they have with each other. Stalin's plan to collectivize farming led to widespread shortages and famine. (© **Margaret Bourke-White/Time & Life Pictures/Getty Images.**)

PEASANT DEATHS UNDER STALIN

14.5 million peasants dead

11 million peasant deaths 1930–1937	6.5 million dead as a result of dekulakization
3.5 million arrested in this period and dying in camps later	1 million dead in Kazakhstan famine of 1932–1933
	7 million dead in famine of 1932–1933:
	5 million in the Ukraine
	1 million in the N. Caucasus
	1 million elsewhere

Taken from: Robert Conquest, *Harvest of Sorrow*. New York: Oxford University Press, 1986.

still in a most unsatisfactory state and it hinders the carrying of the grain and vegetables.

It was the same in old Russia of the Tsar's where there might be grave famine in one region and abundance in another. Today the railways are crowded and goods trains are held up for days, while the food inside the wagons gets bad.

If the trains run badly, food is badly distributed. Vegetables and fruit have to wait days for a train. On Friday October 7th [1930] *Isvestia* [a Russian newspaper] had an example of that: "Last autumn, in the town of Kaluga, mountains of cabbages were being heaped up in the centre of the town in Lenin Square. The green and white pyramids grew bigger and bigger every day. Then it started raining and only when the cabbages began to go rotten was anything done about it. It was taken as fodder for the cattle and to feed the pigs. In a word there was a regular 'cabbage panic' in Kaluga." Such mismanagement is a great hindrance to the fulfillment of the Five-Year Plan.

It is no wonder that the chief organ of the Soviet Government contains news of the shortage of the harvest, that it reports that the grain collections in Ukraine where there has also been a drought [are also short]. North Caucasia and the lower Volga (the chief grain areas) have been exceedingly unsatisfactory and . . . only 40 percent of the July Grain Plan and 60 percent of the August Plan was carried out.

The government paper states that instead [of] 25,000 tons of potatoes the vast Ukraine has only produced 9000. It gives figures showing that the industrial plants such [as] sugar beet . . . [have] only fulfilled a small proportion of the plan.

> In this the last winter of the Five-Year Plan the question will still be: Will there be soup?

It reveals the winter sowing of grain had been in a far lower scale than last year. It shows that the amount of vegetables in the chief towns is disastrously small. It states that shelter is lacking for 1,500,000 head of cattle.

In short it forecasts that in this the last winter of the Five-Year Plan the question will still be: Will there be soup?

Interrogations During the Purges Involved Torture

Bill James

Bill James is a Melbourne, Australia, writer. In the following viewpoint, James discusses the book *The Whisperers: Private Life in Stalin's Russia*. The book, written by Orlando Figes, recounts the experiences of those within the Soviet gulag system of Stalin's era. The most moving part of these accounts, he says, is the story of the children and how they were affected during Stalin's time. Many were left alone to fend for themselves as their parents were imprisoned in the gulags, while others could be punished for their parents' "crimes." Figes also discusses the torture of children as a way to make their parents "confess" during interrogations.

There are many books about different aspects of the Stalin era (1928–53) in the USSR. They include general histories, biographies and studies of specific phenomena such as the Five-Year Plans, the Gulag system, the Great Terror, the Great Patriotic War and the origins of the Cold War.

These are big themes, but there have also been attempts to present life at the grass-roots level, such as Sheila [Fitzpatrick's] *Everyday Stalinism: Ordinary Life in Extraordinary Times: Soviet Russia in the 1930s*, which aimed at describing "extraordinary everydayness", including relationships and family life.

Orlando Figes (whom some *National Observer* readers might have heard reading the poems of Anna Akhmatova in St Paul's Anglican Cathedral during the recent Melbourne Writers' Festival) goes a step further, and considerably deeper. Using primary sources such as diaries, letters and interviews, he brings to light the hidden, unofficial and, in their day, "politically incorrect" interpersonal and interior experiences of Stalin's cowed subjects.

The title refers to the passivity, stoicism and silence which were inculcated in the Soviet population of this era, and which became the conditions of survival. Such communication of sensitive and forbidden subjects as took place, was carried out in whispers. Many children were admonished, "Your mouth will get you into trouble", but many others just absorbed the habit from the adults surrounding them. Informers were ubiquitous.

These habits of fear and reticence were relaxed for many citizens, during the period 1941–5 (when death seemed so constantly imminent that it was harder to terrorise the population), and then again after Stalin's death. In many other cases, however, the obsessive caution persisted for decades after 1953, and in some instances was passed on to the victims' sons and daughters.

> In some cases, children had been prepared by parents, who knew their arrests were imminent, to fend for themselves.

THE DISTRIBUTION OF PRISONERS IN THE GULAG, 1931–1941

Moscow

R U S S I A N   S O V I E T

Number of Prisoners in an Average Year

- 0
- 1–10,000
- 10,001–50,000
- 50,001–100,000
- 100,001–200,000
- 200,001–300,000

FEDERATIVE REPUBLIC

Camp Administration

● With number of prisoners recorded

▲ With no record of prison population

Stories of the Children

Figes's most moving stories concern children. Some involve those with "spoiled biographies", i.e., a noble or "kulak" background, who had to fight discrimination in the areas of education and employment, often by falsifying their origins. Others were orphaned or abandoned during the deliberate famines, or left destitute when parents were arrested, and placed in state children's homes with siblings carefully separated.

In some cases, children had been prepared by parents, who knew their arrests were imminent, to fend for themselves, and even for their little brothers and sisters for whom they suddenly became responsible.

> Worst of all was the torture of children to make parents 'confess'.

Children made prodigious efforts to find parents who had disappeared into the gulag, sometimes locating them after years or decades. The final result of a search was occasionally the discovery that the term "without rights to correspond" on their parents' records, had been Soviet code for "was shot immediately".

The state-sponsored cult of renunciation of parents who were "enemies of the people" saw some children enthusiastically disowning their fathers and mothers. Even worse was Stalin's principle that children (the age of criminal responsibility was reduced to 12 in 1935) could be punished for their parents' crimes. Worst of all was the torture of children to make parents "confess".

Old Bolshevk Stanislav Kosior, a figure hard to sympathise with on any other count, withstood severe mistreatment after his arrest during the Great Terror, but broke down after his teenaged daughter was raped in front of him.

Mothers and fathers, too, travelled huge distances, stood in endless queues, and endured bureaucratic ob-

This photo of Alexandre Soljenitsyne, a Russian author who helped raise international awareness of the gulag, was taken on the day in 1953 when he was released from a forced labor camp. He endured eight years of psychological and physical torture in the gulag. (© **Apic/Getty Images.**)

struction and contempt, in order to find each other and their children.

During the years of forced rural collectivisation, families were arbitrarily classified as "kulaks", uprooted at short notice from villages where their ancestors had lived for centuries, and sent off hundreds or thousands of kilometres with only what they could carry, to live, literally, in holes in the ground.

Conditions in the new industrial cities were not much better. Workers were housed in blocks of flats, two or three families to a vermin-infested apartment with no electricity, running water or sanitation, not to mention privacy.

The Heroism of Mothers

In these circumstances, mothers, especially, fiercely and miraculously maintained some semblance of normal domestic life. Grandmothers, too, emerge time and again as heroic preservers of family stability and cohesion, defying communism's centrifugal tendency to scatter and destroy all normal relationships. Because of their age, they were more resistant to the state's ethically corrosive propaganda, having internalised traditional or liberal moral principles which predated the revolution.

> Sadly, many citizens succumbed to the all-pervasive Stalinist corruption, or allowed their fears to override their innate humanity.

Sadly, many citizens succumbed to the all-pervasive Stalinist corruption, or allowed their fears to override their innate humanity. There are many bleak instances of betrayal, ostracism and exploitation of those who fell foul of the authorities—by spouses, siblings, parents, children, neighbours, colleagues, teachers, erstwhile friends. . . .

Against this background of social disintegration, the examples of loyalty and decency toward pariah victims of the regime, on the part of those who could easily be arrested for assisting an "enemy of the people", stands out with special luminosity.

It is difficult to choose a representative quote from the many on offer, but one in particular illustrates [British author] Paul Johnson's famous line that "An intellectual is a person for whom ideas matter more than people". A woman reminisces about her mother, who started out as an austere and ideologically rigid Bolshevik, but then lived through the Stalin era:

> Could I have ever imagined that my mother, a Party worker, anti-bourgeois and maximalist, who had never allowed herself to use a tender word to me, could turn into a "crazy" grandmother, for whom her grandchildren would be the justification for all the losses of her entire life? Or that she would turn in her Party card with a certain pride and challenge? With that difficult, almost impossible step, she fully gave us her warm, living love, which was higher and greater than abstract ideas and principles.

This [is] a powerful and often emotionally wrenching and moving chronicle. The faces which stare out of the monochrome photos, some torn and crushed, constitute a forceful complement to the text.

In the preface to her *Requiem*, [Russian poet] Anna Akhmatova describes waiting in a queue of prisoners' relatives outside a Moscow jail. "Can you record this?" asked the woman behind her. "I can", she replied.

Figes, too, has been able to distil and immortalise in *The Whisperers* something essential to the record of human experience, for which all civilised people will be grateful.

Doctors Are Put on Trial for an Alleged Plot

Pravda

In the following viewpoint, the official newspaper of the Soviet Communist Party attacks a number of Moscow doctors, most of whom were Jewish. The newspaper claims that the doctors were involved in a plot masterminded by US and Jewish organizations to kill Communist Party leaders with mistreatment. As a result of these accusations, which originated with Joseph Stalin, many Jews were fired, arrested, imprisoned, and executed. Although this viewpoint was written after the time period known as the Great Purge, it provides an example of the Soviet government's tactics. After Stalin died later in 1953, Soviet leadership declared that evidence against the doctors had been fabricated.

Today [January 13, 1953] the TASS news agency reported the arrest of a group of saboteur-doctors. This terrorist group, uncovered some time ago by organs of state security, had as their goal shortening the lives of leaders of the Soviet Union by means of medical sabotage.

Murder Through Mistreatment

Investigation established that participants in the terrorist group, exploiting their position as doctors and abusing the trust of their patients, deliberately and viciously undermined their patients' health by making incorrect diagnoses and then killed them with bad and incorrect treatments. Covering themselves up with the noble and merciful calling of physicians, men of wisdom, these fiends and killers dishonored the holy banner of science. Having taken the path of monstrous crimes, they defiled the honor of scientists.

> Covering themselves up with the noble and merciful calling of physicians, men of wisdom, these fiends and killers dishonored the holy banner of science.

Among the victims of this band of inhuman beasts were [member of the Politburo, the Communist executive committee] Comrades A.A. Zhdanov and A.S. Shcherbakov. The criminals confessed that, taking advantage of the illness of Comrade Zhdanov, they intentionally concealed a myocardial infarction, prescribed inadvisable treatments for this serious illness and thus killed Comrade Zhdanov. Killer doctors, by incorrect use of very powerful medicines and prescription of harmful regimens, shortened the life of Comrade Shcherbakov, leading to his death.

First the criminals tried to undermine the health of the Soviet military leadership cadres, to remove them from the power structure and thereby weaken the defense of the country. The arrest of the criminals disrupted these nefarious plans and prevented the accomplishment of their monstrous goals.

Who did these monsters serve? Who directed the criminal, terrorist, and harmful activity of these vicious traitors to the Motherland? What goal did they want to achieve by the murders of leading figures of the Soviet government?

It has been determined that all participants of the terrorist group of doctors were in the service of foreign intelligence; having sold their bodies and souls, they revealed themselves as hirelings, paid agents.

The majority of the participants of the terrorist group—[Miron] Vovsi, B. Kogan, [A.I.] Feldman, [Alexander] Grinshtein, [Yakov] Etinger and others—were bought by American intelligence agencies. They were recruited by a branch office of American intelligence—the international Jewish bourgeois-nationalist organization called "Joint" [probably the Jewish Joint Distribution Committee, a philanthropic organization]. The filthy face of this Zionist [committed to the establishment of a Jewish nation] spy organization, covering up their vicious actions under the mask of philanthropy, is now completely revealed.

Terrorists Unmasked

Relying upon a group of corrupt Jewish bourgeois nationalists, the professional spies and terrorists of "Joint," through assignments from and under the direction of American intelligence, extended their subversive activity even into the territory of the Soviet Union. As the prisoner Vovsi revealed under interrogation, he received directives "about the extermination of leadership cadres of the USSR," from the USA. These instructions were handed to him, in the name of the spy-terrorist "Joint" organization, through Dr. [Boris] Shimeliovich and the well-known Jewish bourgeois nationalist [Solomon] Mikhoels.

> Unmasking the gang of poisoner-doctors struck a blow against the international Jewish Zionist organization.

Unmasking the gang of poisoner-doctors struck a blow against the international Jewish Zionist organization. Now all can see what sort of "philanthropists" and "friends of peace" were hiding under the label of "Joint."

Other participants in the terrorist group ([Stalin's physician Vladimir] Vinogradov, M. Kogan, [Mitali] Egorov) were discovered, as has been presently determined, to have been long-time agents of English intelligence, serving it for many years and carrying out its most criminal and sordid tasks. The bigwigs of the USA and their English junior partners know that to achieve domination over other nations by peaceful means is impossible. Feverishly preparing for a new world war, they energetically send spies inside the USSR and the people's democratic countries: they attempt to accomplish what the Hitlerites could not do—to create within the USSR their own subversive "fifth column." It is enough to recall the undisguised and cynical appropriation by the American government of $100,000,000 for subversive terror and espionage activity in countries belonging to the socialist camp, to say nothing of the hundreds of millions of dollars, American and English, which are being spent in secret for this purpose.

The Soviet people must not for a minute forget about the need to heighten their vigilance in all ways possible, to keep a sharp eye out for all schemes of warmongers and their agents, and to constantly strengthen the Armed Forces and the intelligence organs of our government.

Comrade [Joseph] Stalin has repeatedly warned that our successes have their dark side, that they cause among many of our workers a spirit of placidity and complacency. These sorts of moods are far from being overcome. We still have many complacent people. It is exactly this heedlessness of our people that is fertile soil for villainous sabotage.

In the USSR, socialist relations rule completely. In the Great Patriotic War, the Soviet people won a victory which is unparalleled in history. In an unprecedentedly short period of time, the dire consequences of war have been liquidated. In all areas of economic and cultural construction, we have successes. From these facts, certain people have drawn the conclusion that now the dangers of wrecking, sabotage, and espionage have disappeared, that the bosses of the capitalist world will give up their attempts to conduct subversive activities against the USSR.

But only Right-Opportunists can think and reason this way, people standing for an anti-Marxist view of the "decay" of the class struggle. They do not or cannot understand that our successes lead not to "decay," but to intensification of the struggle. The more successful our progress forward, the fiercer will be the strife of the enemies of the people who are doomed to destruction and driven to despair.

This the immortal [Vladimir] Lenin teaches, this Comrade Stalin teaches.

"In our revolution," Lenin points out, "more than in any other, this law was proven: that as the strength of the revolution and the intensity of its power, energy, determination, and celebration of its victory increase, so too will the opposition from the bourgeoisie."

Denouncing the opportunistic theory of the "decaying" class struggle due to the degree of our success, Comrade Stalin warned:

"This is not only a rotten theory, but is also a dangerous theory, because it lulls our people to sleep, leads them into a trap, and gives the class enemy a chance to mount war against Soviet power."

Bourgeois Ideology Remains

In the USSR the exploiting classes were broken up and liquidated a long time ago, but still there remain vestiges of bourgeois ideology, vestiges of the morality and psychology of private ownership. There remain bearers of bourgeois views and bourgeois morals, [who are] living people, hidden enemies of our nation. It is exactly these

Photo on opposite page: Andrei Alexandrovich Zhdanov, a physician and former Communist Party official in Leningrad, was one of the doctors falsely accused of perpetrating a plot to kill party officials. (© Bettmann/ Corbis.)

hidden enemies, supported by the imperialistic world, who will be harmful in the future.

All this obliges the Soviet people in every possible way to strengthen their revolutionary vigilance and to keep a sharp eye out for enemy plots. The fact that a group of filthy degenerates from the ranks of "men of science" were able to work for some time with impunity, reveals how some of our Soviet organs and leaders lost their vigilance, having been infected with the virus of carelessness.

> All this obliges the Soviet people . . . to strengthen their revolutionary vigilance and to keep a sharp eye out for enemy plots.

The organs of State Security did not expose in a timely fashion the subversive, terrorist organization among the doctors. These organs should have been especially watchful, because history already knows of cases where base murderers and traitors to the Motherland operated under the mask of physicians, such as "Doctors" [Lev] Levin and [Dmitry] Pletnev.[1] These "doctors," on a mission for enemies of the Soviet Union, killed by administering deliberately improper treatments [to] the great Russian author A.M. Gorky and prominent members of the Soviet government V.V. Kujbyshev and V.R. Menzhinsky.

Nor were the leaders of the Ministry of Public Health up to the task. They overlooked the subversive terrorist activity of the vile degenerates, who had sold out to the enemies of the Soviet Union.

The exposure of the gang of poisoner-doctors is a shattering blow against the Anglo-American warmongers. Their agents were captured and neutralized. Once again the true face of the slaveholding ogres of the USA and England was revealed before the whole world.

With anger and indignation the Soviet people denounce this criminal band of killers and their foreign bosses. The despicable hirelings who serve for dollars and sterling will be crushed like a loathsome snake. The masterminds of these hired killers can be certain they will not escape punishment. The people's retribution will find them, denouncing them with its profound judgment.

All this is true, of course. But it is also true that, apart from these enemies, we have still one more: the lack of vigilance of our people. It cannot be doubted that as long as we aren't paying attention, there will be sabotage. Therefore to eliminate sabotage we must purge lack of vigilance from our ranks.

Note

1. Levin and Pletnev were tried as part of a major show trial in 1938.

Stalin's Successor Denounces Stalin and the Purges

Nikita Khrushchev

In the following viewpoint, Stalin's successor, Nikita Khrushchev, delivers a speech to a closed session of the Communist Party in 1956. He denounces Stalin and his policies of terror. He argues that Stalin set himself up as a leader above the law in violation of Communist principles. He also says that Stalin illegally forced confessions, imprisoned, and executed political rivals and enemies. Though delivered in secret, his speech soon became public knowledge. The revelation of Stalin's crimes shocked people both in the Soviet Union and abroad. Khrushchev was a high-ranking member of Stalin's inner circle who became the leader of the Soviet Union after Stalin's death in 1953.

SOURCE. Nikita Khrushchev, "The Secret Speech—On the Cult of Personality, 1956," *Congressional Record: Proceedings and Debates of the 84th Congress, 2nd Session* (May 22–June 11, 1956), vol. 11, no. 7, pp. 9389–9403.

[Joseph] Stalin acted not through persuasion, explanation, and patient cooperation with people, but by imposing his concepts and demanding absolute submission to his opinion. Whoever opposed this concept or tried to prove his viewpoint, and the correctness of his position—was doomed to removal from the leading collective and to subsequent moral and physical annihilation. This was especially true during the period following the 17th party congress [in 1934] when many prominent party leaders and rank-and-file party workers, honest and dedicated to the cause of communism, fell victim to Stalin's despotism. . . .

Mass Repression

Stalin originated the concept enemy of the people. This term automatically rendered it unnecessary that the ideological errors of a man or men engaged in a controversy be proven; this term made possible the usage of the most cruel repression, violating all norms of revolutionary legality, against anyone who in any way disagreed with Stalin, against those who were only suspected of hostile intent, against those who had bad reputations. This concept, enemy of the people, actually eliminated the possibility of any kind of ideological fight or the making of one's views known on this or that issue, even those of a practical character. In the main, and in actuality, the only proof of guilt used, against all norms of current legal science, was the confession of the accused himself, and, as subsequent probing proved, confessions were acquired through physical pressures against the accused. . . .

[Vladimir] Lenin [the first leader of the Soviet Union] used severe methods only in the most necessary cases, when the exploiting classes were still in existence and were vigorously opposing the revolution, when the struggle for survival was decidedly assuming the sharpest forms, even including a civil war.

Khrushchev Delivers the Secret Speech

Many in the audience were unreconstructed Stalinists; those who had denounced former colleagues and clambered over their corpses suddenly feared for their own heads. Others, who had secretly hated [Joseph] Stalin, couldn't believe his successor [Nikita Khrushchev] was joining their ranks. As the KGB [the Soviet secret service] chief-to-be Vladimir Semichastny remembered it, the speech was at first met with "a deathly silence; you could hear a bug fly by." When the noise started, it was a tense, muffled hum. Zakhar Glukhov, Khrushchev's successor in Petrovo-Marinsky near Donetsk, felt "anxious and joyous at the same time" and marveled at how Khrushchev "could have brought himself to say such things before such an audience." Dmitri Goriunov, the chief editor of *Komsomolskaya pravda* [an official Communist paper], took five nitroglycerin pills for a weak heart. "We didn't look each other in the eye as we came down from the balcony," recalled Aleksandr Yakovlev, then a minor functionary for the Central Committee Propaganda Department . . . , "whether from shame or shock or from the simple unexpectedness of it, I don't know." As the delegates left the hall, all Yakovlev heard them muttering was "*Da-a, da-a, da-a,*" as if compressing all the intense, conflicting emotions they felt in the single, safe word, "yes."

Khrushchev spoke with "agitation and emotion," [Central Committee official Igor] Chernoutsan remembered, his speech peppered with explosive asides—"the most interesting things he said," according to Yakovlev—that never made it into the official transcript that found its way to the West in 1956 and wasn't published in the USSR until 1989. His hatred for Stalin was particularly visible when he held him accountable for the disastrous Kiev and Kharkov defeats in 1941 and 1942 [World War II]. "It burst forth," according to Chernoutsan, "when he cried out in fury, 'He [Stalin] was a coward. He panicked. Not once during the whole war did he dare go to the front.'"

SOURCE: *William Taubman,* Khrushchev: The Man and His Era. *New York: W.W. Norton & Co., 2003, p. 273.*

Stalin, on the other hand, used extreme methods and mass repressions at a time when the revolution was already victorious, when the Soviet state was strengthened, when the exploiting classes were already liquidated, and

Socialist relations were rooted solidly in all phases of national economy, when our party was politically consolidated and had strengthened itself both numerically and ideologically. It is clear that here Stalin showed in a whole series of cases his intolerance, his brutality, and his abuse of power. Instead of proving his political correctness and mobilizing the masses, he often chose the path of repression and physical annihilation, not only against actual enemies, but also against individuals who had not committed any crimes against the party and the Soviet Government. Here we see no wisdom but only a demonstration of the brutal force which had once so alarmed V.I. Lenin. . . .

> "Stalin showed in a whole series of cases his intolerance, his brutality, and his abuse of power."

Stalin Ruled Alone

Considering the question of the cult of an individual we must first of all show everyone what harm this caused to the interests of our party. . . .

In practice Stalin ignored the norms of party life and trampled on the Leninist principle of collective party leadership.

Stalin's willfulness vis-a-vis the party and its central committee became fully evident after the 17th party congress, which took place in 1934. . . .

It was determined that of the 139 members and candidates of the party's Central Committee who were elected at the 17th congress, 98 persons, that is, 70 percent, were arrested and shot (mostly in 1937–38). [Indignation in the hall.] . . .

The same fate met not only the central committee members but also the majority of the delegates to the 17th party congress. Of 1,966 delegates with either voting or advisory rights, 1,108 persons were arrested on charges of anti-revolutionary crimes, i.e., decidedly more than a majority. This very fact shows how absurd, wild, and contrary to commonsense were the charges of counter-revolutionary crimes made out, as we now see, against a majority of participants at the 17th party congress. [Indignation in the hall.] . . .

> Stalin had so elevated himself above the party and above the nation that he ceased to consider either the central committee or the party.

What is the reason that mass repressions against activists increased more and more after the 17th party congress? It was because at that time Stalin had so elevated himself above the party and above the nation that he ceased to consider either the central committee or the party. While he still reckoned with the opinion of the collective before the 17th congress, after the complete political liquidation of the Trotskyites, Zinovievites and Bukharinites,[1] when as a result of that fight and Socialist victories the party achieved unity, Stalin ceased to an ever greater degree to consider the members of the party's central committee and even the members of the Political Bureau. Stalin thought that now he could decide all things alone and all he needed were statisticians; he treated all others in such a way that they could only listen to and praise him.

After the criminal murder of S.M. Kirov,[2] mass repressions and brutal acts of violation of Socialist legality began. On the evening of December 1, 1934, on Stalin's initiative (without the approval of the Political Bureau—which was passed 2 days later, casually) the Secretary of the Presidium of the Central Executive Committee, [Avel] Yenukidze, signed the following directive:

I. Investigative agencies are directed to speed up the cases of those accused of the preparation or execution of acts of terror.

II. Judicial organs are directed not to hold up the execution of death sentences pertaining to crimes of

this category in order to consider the possibility of pardon, because the Presidium of the Central Executive Committee, U.S.S.R., does not consider as possible the receiving of petitions of this sort.

III. The organs of the Commissariat of Internal Affairs are directed to execute the death sentences against criminals of the above-mentioned category immediately after the passage of sentences.

This directive became the basis for mass acts of abuse against Socialist legality. During many of the fabricated court cases the accused were charged with "the preparation" of terroristic acts; this deprived them of any possibility that their cases might be reexamined, even when they stated before the court that their confessions were secured by force, and when, in a convincing manner, they disproved the accusations against them. . . .

Now when the cases of some of these so-called spies and saboteurs were examined it was found that all their

Under a massive statue of Vladimir Lenin, Nikita Khrushchev (left foreground) addresses the Central Committee of the Communist Party of the Soviet Union in 1956. Later that year he would denounce Stalin to the same group. (© **Gino Mercatali/Mondadori via Getty Images**.)

cases were fabricated. Confessions of guilt of many—arrested and charged with enemy activity were gained with the help of cruel and inhuman tortures.

Notes

1. The Trotskyites, Zinovievites, and Bukharinites are all factions within the Communist Party.
2. Sergei Kirov was an early Soviet leader. He was assassinated in 1934.

CHAPTER 2

Controversies Surrounding Stalin's Great Purge

The Purge Was a Rational Response to Corruption in the Communist Party

Mário Sousa

In the following viewpoint, the author argues that Western anti-Communist writers have misrepresented the purges. He maintains that purges during the early 1930s were mostly intended to purify the Communist Party. He argues that these purges were performed in good faith and without terror. He says that purges in the later 1930s were done in the shadow of the threat from Nazi Germany, when the Soviet Union was threatened by internal traitors. He concludes that the purges, trials, and executions were necessary to ensure the survival of the Soviet Union and the defeat of Adolf Hitler's Germany. Mário Sousa is a Swedish Communist writer.

Photo on previous page: The ruins of a gulag prison in Siberia are nearly covered over by the typical heavy snowfalls of the area. Prisoners endured severe conditions in these prisons, which were used to suppress political dissent. (© Arctic-Images/Corbis.)

SOURCE. Mário Sousa, "The Class Struggle During the Thirties in the Soviet Union," mariosousa.se, 2001. Copyright © 2001 by Mário Sousa. All rights reserved. Reproduced by permission.

The purges of, or expulsions from, the Soviet communist party and the political trials in Moscow during the 1930s are two of the favourite issues for the bourgeois [the class of property owners] propagandists. They are brought up time and time again in bourgeois mass media, giving the public a completely untruthful and false picture of the purges, the political trials and the Soviet Union of the period. Their purpose is to defame socialism and the Soviet Union to prevent people of today from listening to the communists and make them accept capitalism as something inevitable. For that reason it is important to clarify this chapter of the history of the Soviet Union. This [is] in order both to fight the bourgeois lies and to understand the difficulty which the Bolsheviks met in the revolutionary transition. Recent historical research has been carried out in this area, and that is one of the bases for the article. For the rest, literature and documents from the 1930s and the 1940s are used, which long ago have fallen into oblivion or totally unknown by most people. . . .

Purges During the 1920s

After the victory of the revolution, when the Communist party had become the ruling party, the party leadership and Lenin had to acknowledge that some unwelcome elements had penetrated into the party and state apparatus. They were people who wanted to make a career via a membership in the party. At the eighth party conference in December of 1919 Lenin brought this problem up. According to Lenin . . . "It is natural, on the one hand, that all the worst elements should cling to the ruling party merely because it is the ruling party". For that reason it was important to evaluate the contribution of the party members. On the proposal of Lenin, the party carried out a re-registration of all party members. Every member had to answer for his actions in front of the member collective—those who were considered unreliable were excluded. That was the first purification of the party apparatus. This method, to strengthen the party by purging the opportunistic elements, was to characterise the Communist party for many years to come.

> The general criteria for the purging of party members were corruption, passivity, breaches of party discipline, alcoholism, criminality and anti-Semitism.

The general criteria for the purging of party members were corruption, passivity, breaches of party discipline, alcoholism, criminality and anti-Semitism. For bourgeois individuals and kulaks [wealthy peasants] who hid their class origin, expulsion was certain. (But not for those who had been accepted into the party and who had admitted their class background.) For the former tsarist officers [officers of the Czar, the former Russian ruler] who hid their past were also inevitably expelled. All those who had been expelled could in their turn appeal to the Central control commission, and then their cases were reviewed at a higher level.

As we shall see later, a relatively high number got their party membership back. The decisions at the general meetings with hundreds of members were, as a rule, more rigid than those at the party centre. The Central Committee of the party, which had initiated the purges and decided their forms, tried first to make the members at the base level to speak out and clamp down on corrupt functionaries and their companions.

This turned out to be difficult work. Corrupt bureaucrats knew thousands of tricks to escape criticism and tricky situations. Instead, the majority of those expelled were base level members who often could not defend themselves against the accusations by the party secretaries for passivity, political ignorance or bad drinking habits.

After the re-registration of 1919 Lenin and the party leadership found that there were still considerable shortcomings in the party. The re-registration had not

THE EXPULSIONS OF 1933	
Reason for Expulsion	Percent
Moral corruption, careerist, bureaucrat	17.5
Alien elements / hiding alien past	16.5
Violation of party discipline	20.9
Passivity	23.2
Other	17.9

Taken from: J. Arch Getty, *Origins of the Great Purges: The Soviet Communist Party Reconsidered*, 1933–1938. New York: Cambridge University Press, 1987, p. 54.

achieved its aim. A great number of new members continued to be drawn into the party without consideration to the directive of electing only workers and reliable elements from other classes. New purges took place [in] 1921, 1928 and 1929. . . .

In relation to the purges of 1929, there is a detailed description of the causes. It does in fact provide good information and does away with at least [one] myth—that the purges would have been a way to get rid of opposing elements within the party. In 1929, 1.53 million party members went through the process of purges. Of these approx. 170,000 or 11 per cent were expelled. When they appealed to the Central control commission 37,000 got their party membership back (22 per cent of those expelled). In Smolensk, as many as 43 per cent of those expelled got their party membership back. When they were further examined, it turns out that the great majority were base members from the working class, who had been expelled by the local party functionaries for passivity. No regard had been taken to the living conditions which made it more difficult for these members to take part in the party activities. . . .

The Purges During the 1930s

Let us now pass to the Soviet Union of the 1930s. The purges during the 1930s are precisely what is always brought forth by those who want to defame socialism and reinforce the myth of the Soviet Union as an oppressive state. Among the most famous falsifiers of history we find the former police agent of the British secret service, Robert Conquest [a British historian], the fascist Alexander Solsjenitsyn [a Russian writer who spent time in the gulag] and the Russian social democrat Roy Medvedev. . . .

The Purges of 1933

During the 1930s the party underwent three great purges: 1933, 1935 and 1937–1938. The first purge [in] 1933 took part in a clime of great enthusiasm in society when the agricultural cooperatives spread all over the Soviet Union with great steps forward, and the industrial production attained results never before seen. The party had opened its doors for all who wanted to fight for socialism and hundreds of thousands new members had been elected during the first three years of the 1930s. Because of the great onslaught, the party leadership considered it a necessity to evaluate the new party members. They were seeking opportunists, corrupt bureaucrats, criminals, anti-Semites, alcoholics or members violating party discipline.

> "The party directives clarified that the purges should take place in a comradely atmosphere not allowing any deep digging into people's private lives.

The party directives clarified that the purges should take place in a comradely atmosphere not allowing any deep digging into people's private lives. Moreover, the party leadership encouraged base members to be openly critical against the local bureaucrats and warned the local party leaderships against expelling base members for passivity or political ignorance. The mistakes of 1929 were not to be repeated. Attention should be paid to the general development of members and in those cases it was deemed necessary party members could be degraded to candidates or sympathisers until they had improved their political knowledge or increased their participation in the activities of the party. Expulsion should be avoided as far as possible.

In spite of the directives, the purge of 1933 turned out differently from what the Central Committee had intended. In a country so vast as the Soviet Union the local party secretaries had a great power, which sometimes proved fatal. Facts show that local party secretaries did their best to avoid criticism from striking them or their near ones. Just in order to demonstrate their interest in a successful purge, some local secretaries threw out many base members, workers and farmers; faithful members, precisely the ones who should not have been expelled. The majority of those expelled were people who had entered the party between 1930 and 1933, who had not had time to get knowledge of all the party issues. Many had not been able to study the party programme at depth and Marxism-Leninism, and they were regarded to be all too ignorant by the party secretaries. Others were people who had difficulties in taking full part in party life because of their work situation or family problems. During the purge of 1933 18.5 per cent of party members and candidates were expelled. . . .

The purge of 1933, which was terminated in the middle of 1934, revealed a serious contradiction within the party. The Central Committee wanted to throw out thieves and corrupt bureaucrats, but the biggest group expelled—in fact almost one fourth—were expelled for passivity. Passivity did not figure among the party directives as a criterion for expulsion. With the assistance of bureaucratic methods or authority gained for earlier merits, local party leaders [did] whatever they wanted

Grigory Evseevitch Zinoviev (standing, top left) was a political rival of Joseph Stalin and one of the first to be prosecuted during the so-called Moscow Trials. (© **Hulton Archive/ Getty Images.**)

without paying attention to the directives of the Central Committee. The extension of the antagonisms is implied by the one fourth expelled for passivity. The Central Committee had to do something about the local party leaders' contravention of the party directives, but as the future was to show, it was not very easy. This became very timely during the following years when the Soviet Union was forced to increase the pace of development to survive.

Another aspect of the statistics found by [US historian J. Arch] Getty concerns the allegation by Conquest and other rightists that the purge of 1933 was organised to throw out old Bolsheviks—old party cadres from the days of Lenin—who had come into opposition with Stalin. According to Getty, the allegation is improbable.

The great majority by far of those expelled, two thirds in fact, had entered the party after 1928 and were for that reason to be considered relatively new party members. The distribution of those expelled as 23 per cent agricultural workers/farmers, 14.6 per cent civil servants and approx. 62 per cent workers shows, that the overwhelming majority, 85 per cent, were ordinary working men rather than party cadres from Lenin's time. In *The Great Terror* Robert Conquest touches upon the purge of 1933 and hints that over a million members were expelled for political reasons. If one has knowledge of the history of the purges, it becomes evident that Conquest's allegation is a lie. . . .

The Political Trials of 1936–1938 in the Soviet Union

The political trials and the purges in the Communist party were two separate things which did not directly have anything to do with each other. The party members who were expelled and tried at court for having been involved in criminal or counter revolutionary activities were a small minority of all those who were expelled. In order to understand this, it is important to know the history of the political trials during the 1930s. Bourgeois history writings exclude such possibilities. They have made the events of the 1930s into a totally confused story and a grossly falsified mixture of happenings and myths, lies and half-truths, a falsification which presents the purges and the treason trials as the same one occurrence.

The political trials were started by the trial against the [Leon] Trotsky-[Grigory] Zinoviev[1] centre in August 1936, the first of four between 1936 and 1938. In bourgeois mass media they are usually called the Moscow trials and are always depicted as macabre histories of "Stalin's revenge", whereby millions of people were dragged from their homes in the middle of the night to be killed in the most dire circumstances imaginable. According to the book by Peter Englund *Letters from Point Zero* they were killed by shots in the neck in "soundproof" rooms with a "tarpaulin" on the floor or "grooves sunk into the floor like the ones to be seen in slaughterhouses". According to him, "the corpses were freighted away" by people "dressed in dark protective coats, aprons, rubber gloves and meat hooks" and were thrown up "on a truck where other undressed corpses were lying and waited". The trucks were running in a shuttle traffic, according to Englund, and they left traces of dripping bloods in the streets of Moscow.

Englund's stories have been taken from Conquest and writers paid by the CIA. Englund himself is an ignorant wretch, who has no ambition to give the Swedish readers knowledge of what really happened in the Soviet Union during the 1930s. For good pay he happily lends his name to any attacks against Socialism and the Soviet Union.

> "Hundreds of saboteurs, spies and all kinds of traitors were condemned to prison or death."

In the so called Moscow trials 55 people got capital punishment and 7 imprisonment. Most of those prosecuted were persons in high positions in the party, the state apparatus and the army accused of treason, espionage, terrorism, sabotage, corruption or collaboration with the enemy, Nazi Germany [as World War II approached]. The Moscow trials were followed by trials in other parts of the country against companions of the traitors tried in Moscow, and hundreds of saboteurs, spies and all kinds of traitors were condemned to prison or death. The trials were public except trials against military personnel, which were held behind closed doors because of the secrecy in the defence preparations against Nazi Germany. In Moscow the trials were monitored by the international press and the accredited diplomatic corps, for which seats were reserved in the court room. Minutes from the three public Moscow trials were published as books by the Soviet government and translated into many languages, Swedish among others. . . .

The Traitors and the Threat Against the Soviet Union

Those who browse through ordinary daily newspapers from the 1930s can easily see how the threat against the Soviet Union grew from one day to the other. The threat came from Nazi Germany but from the other capitalist countries in the West too, among others from France and Great Britain. It went on like that during the entire 1930s. When the Nazis invaded Poland in September 1939 France and Great Britain declared war against Germany but did not undertake any acts of war nor tried to save Poland. It was the so called "fanny war". The real war between France/Great Britain and Nazi Germany did not start until nine months later with the invasion by the Nazis of France in June 1940. But during the period September 1939–June 1940, France and Great Britain were not passive.

The anti-Soviet policies dominated in these countries. In France an Ukrainian legion was created with defectors from the Soviet Union and national combat units of Caucasians in the army of the French general [Maxime] Weygand. When Finland started the war against the Soviet Union in December 1939 France and Great Britain took position on Finland's side. Great Britain sent 144 war planes, 114 heavy guns and hundreds of thousands of grenades and air bombs. France sent 179 war planes, 472 guns, 5,100 machine guns and approx. one million grenades. . . . Simultaneously these countries made up plans to send in an army of 150,000 men to fight on the Finnish side against the Soviet Union. The governments of France and Great Britain wanted to show Nazi Germany where they belonged. The massive threat against the Soviet Union was evident during all of the 1930s. Everywhere in capitalist Europe the governments prepared the public opinion for a war against the Soviet Union. There, this threat was perceived as real.

The soviet leadership had to realise that the country would perish unless they managed in uniting everybody in the work for a quick development of the society and the enormous necessary defence preparations which absorbed a large part of the social production. In this strained social climate the soviet government discovered that the countries threatening the Soviet Union had their own mercenaries inside the countries, connections reaching high up in the state and the party. In this very strained situation where everybody had to work very hard for the survival of the Soviet Union, there were others who helped the enemy with information and sabotaged the production and the defence.

> It is unfortunate if innocent people were affected. But in the prevailing situation there was nothing better to do.

The Soviet government was hard on the traitors and the circles all over the Soviet Union where these traitors moved or had connections. Many were condemned to prison or to death. . . . It is unfortunate if innocent people were affected. But in the prevailing situation there was nothing better to do. The Nazi invasion and the war of extermination against the Soviet Union was fast approaching. For the administration and state apparatus it would be suicide to retain people who were prepared to collaborate with the Nazi invaders and who were inimical against the Socialist State. With their powerful actions the Soviet government succeeded in saving the country—and the world—from the Nazi barbary and to eradicate Nazism. How would history have judged the Soviet government if the Soviet Union had perished and the Nazis taken over the whole world?

Note

1. Trotsky and Zinoviev were Communist rivals of Stalin.

The Purge Was a Means for Stalin to Ruthlessly Solidify Power

Rob Sewell

In the following viewpoint, Marxist writer Rob Sewell says that the Soviet purges were a means for Stalin to eliminate his rivals, especially Leon Trotsky. The author maintains that Trotsky stayed true to the original ideals of the Russian Revolution. He argues that those ideals, and Trotsky's personal leadership, were a real threat to Stalin's bureaucratic totalitarianism. Stalin targeted old Bolshevik Communist leaders who could challenge his power and who might support Trotsky. The author concludes that Stalin was a traitor to the revolution, and the purges were a way to destroy those who remained true to its ideals.

The Great Purge and Terror were launched by [Joseph] Stalin not because he was insane. On the contrary, it was a conscious, well-prepared course of action to safe-guard the rule of the bureaucracy. Stalin arrived at the decision to destroy the 'Old Bolsheviks'[1] not later than the summer of 1934, and then began to prepare his operation—beginning with the murder of [the early Bolshevik leader Sergei] Kirov in December of that year.

The Bureaucracy

[Bolshevik leader Leon] Trotsky explained Stalin's actions:

> It is time, my listeners, it is high time, to recognise, finally, that a new aristocracy has been formed in the Soviet Union. The October Revolution [the 1917 Russian Revolution] proceeded under the banner of equality. The bureaucracy is the embodiment of monstrous inequality. The revolution destroyed the nobility. The bureaucracy creates a new gentry. The revolution destroyed titles and decorations. The new aristocracy produces marshals and generals. The new aristocracy absorbs an enormous part of the national income. Its position before the people is deceitful and false. Its leaders are forced to hide the reality, to deceive the masses, to cloak themselves, calling black white. The whole policy of the new aristocracy is a frame-up.

The situation by 1934 was giving rise for alarm amongst the Stalinist bureaucracy. There was profound discontent throughout the country after the debacle of forced collectivisation [of agriculture] and the adventure of the first Five Year Plan [for Soviet economic development]. Opposition moods were wide-spread. Stalin feared that the Old Bolsheviks—although forced to repeatedly capitulate to Stalin—would become a focal point for opposition. Some had in fact made contact with Trotsky in exile.

Stalin used the assassination of Kirov to launch his plans. Originally the perpetrators of the murder were declared to be a group of 13 'Zinovievists', shot in December 1934. The former oppositionists [Grigory]

Zinoviev and [Les] Kamenev—who had had earlier broken with Trotsky and capitulated—were then convicted in January 1935 with 'objectively' inflaming terrorist moods amongst their supporters. But this was only the beginning.

Stalin now realised his mistake in exiling Trotsky in 1928, which allowed him to freely criticise the Stalinist regime from abroad. Trotsky was the most important focal point of opposition to Stalin. He was a revolutionary leader that would not be broken. From then on Stalin prepared his assassination. Consequently, Stalin set about the frame-up of Trotsky and his supporters on charges of terrorism.

Confessions

This job was given to the NKVD [the Soviet secret police] under [Genrikh] Yagoda and then [Nikolai] Yezhov, both Stalinist hangmen. They had to 'prove' the existence of an underground terrorist Zinoviev organisation which collaborated with [a] secret Trotskyist network. In early 1935 a directive was given to the NKVD which demanded the 'total liquidation of the entire Trotsky-Zinoviev underground'. Arrests took place of suspected oppositionists and former-oppositionists. Then followed the interrogations and first 'confessions'—receiving terrorist orders from Trotsky.

After a year and a half in prison, Zinoviev and Kamenev were brought to Moscow for their interrogation. They had been repeatedly broken—morally crushed—by this time. As was Stalin's method, he had managed to sow mutual discord between the two men. Zinoviev wrote Stalin grovelling letters from his cell: 'My soul burns with one desire: to prove to you that I am no longer an enemy. There is no demand which I would not fullfil in order to prove this. . .'

Kamenev bore himself with particular courage. He told his interrogator: 'You are now observing Thermidor

Leon Trotsky

Leon Trotsky (Lev Davidovich Trotskii [Bronshtein]) was a leading Russian revolutionary. Born into a Jewish farming family in present-day Ukraine, Trotsky became a Marxist publicist and organizer in the 1890s. During Russia's 1905 Revolution, he became chairman of the St. Petersburg Soviet of Workers' Deputies just before its suppression by the tsarist government. Forced to flee Russia, he spent the next several years as a journalist in Europe.

After 1917's February Revolution overthrew the tsarist regime, Trotsky returned to Russia. Despite fifteen years of disputes with Vladimir Lenin, Trotsky now found their views congruent, and joined Lenin's Bolsheviks to help lead the October coup d'état that overthrew Russia's provisional government. Trotsky served briefly as Soviet foreign minister before shifting in spring 1918 to building the Soviet military to fight the Russian civil war. After the Red Army's 1920 victory, Trotsky struggled against other Bolsheviks to take the ailing Lenin's place as head of the Soviet Union. For some historically conscious Bolsheviks, Trotsky's talent, military authority, and arrogance raised the specter of a new Bonaparte; a coalition of enemies, led by Joseph Stalin, first removed him from power then exiled him in 1929. . . .

Trotsky did not attribute his defeat to Stalin, who he dismissed as a nonentity, but instead to Russian backwardness. Material want and a scarcity of class-conscious workers, Trotsky argued, created

Arriving in Mexico in 1937, Leon Trotsky (second from right) and his wife (far left) are greeted by artist Frida Kahlo and American Communist leader Max Schachtman. Dissidents such as Trotsky where forced into exile but were welcomed by artists and leaders of other countries. (© Bettmann/Corbis.)

the conditions for the ascendance of the Soviet bureaucracy, which employed Stalin as a tool to solidify its own position. . . .

Trotsky's opposition to Stalin led to his assassination in 1940 by a Stalinist agent in Mexico City.

SOURCE: *David R. Stone, "Trotsky, Leon,"* International Encyclopedia of the Social Sciences, *vol. 8, 2nd ed. Detroit: Macmillan Reference USA, 2008, pp. 455–456.*

[a period of terror during the French Revolution] in a pure form. The French Revolution taught us a good lesson, but we weren't able to put it to use. We don't know how to protect our revolution from Thermidor. That is our greatest mistake, and history will condemn us for it.'

Yezhov was ordered to prepare them for a public trial, and that they should slander themselves and Trotsky—for the sake of the revolution! Threats were made against their families, a number of whom were held by the NKVD. They were incarcerated and subjected to humiliating procedures. Zinoviev was the first to break, who then persuaded Kamenev to follow suite in return for their lives and those of their families and supporters. They were then brought before Stalin and [Kliment] Voroshilov. Zinoviev pleaded with them: 'You want to depict members of Lenin's Politburo and Lenin's personal friends to be unprincipled bandits, and present the party as a snake's nest of intrigue, treachery and murderers.' To this Stalin replied that the Trial was not aimed at them, but against Trotsky, 'the sworn enemy of the Party.'

> "Stalin betrayed them, as he would betray the rest. It was in reality a betrayal of the Revolution.

Their pleas for their lives were met with Stalin's vow that all this 'goes without saying.' Stalin betrayed them, as he would betray the rest. It was in reality a betrayal of the Revolution in the interests of the ruling bureaucracy at whose head was Stalin.

[Ivan] Smirnov and [Sergei] Mrachkovsky both stubbornly refused to give confessions to the interrogators. According to the chief prosecutor, [Andrey] Vyshinsky, Smirnov's entire interrogation on 20 May consisted of his words: 'I deny this. I deny it once again. I deny it.' Mrachkovsky was taken before Stalin personally, but rejected his advances. He was then handed over to [Abram] Slutsky, head of the NKVD's foreign department. According to him, he interrogated Mrachkovsky non-stop for almost four days. Mrachkovsky told Slutsky: 'You can tell Stalin that I hate him. He is a traitor. They took me to Molotov, who also wanted to buy me off. I spit in his face.' During the interrogation every two hours the phone rang from Stalin's secretary to ask whether he had managed to 'break' Mrachkovsky. After a lengthy interrogation he finally broke down in tears 'concluding everything was lost.' For a long time he refused to smear Trotsky with terrorist activity.

Trial of the Sixteen

The first show Trial—the Trial of the Sixteen—sought to destroy the mythical Trotsky-Zinoviev Centre. Vyshinsky did not provide a shred of evidence against the accused—not one document, not a scrap of paper—only the confessions of the accused. The weakness of the prosecutor's case was demonstrated by the inconsistencies and falsehoods in the testimonies given at the trial. [E.S.] Goltsman, for instance, testified he met Trotsky and Sedov in Copenhagen at the Hotel Bristol. Unbeknown to the prosecutors, the Hotel Bristol had been demolished in 1917! The Stalinist investigators had not done their homework.

At the conclusion of the Trial, Vyshinsky for the prosecution declared: 'I demand that we shoot the mad dogs—every single one of them!' Despite the pleas for mercy submitted by the Sixteen—which they were led to believe would be honoured—within a matter of hours they were taken out and shot.

> 'Stalin needs Trotsky's head—this is his main goal.'

Those who grovelled before the Stalinist dictatorship—throwing all kinds of slanders against their former comrades—could never satisfy Stalin. They would be eliminated after their allotted role was complete. New amalgams were being prepared. New Witch Trials would take place. As Leon

Sedov explained: 'Stalin needs Trotsky's head—this is his main goal. To achieve it he will launch the most extreme and even more insidious cases.'

With the collapse of Hitler Germany in 1945 and the Nuremberg Trials, which laid bare the Nazi regime and their collaborators, not one word or document was found to prove the slightest connection between Trotsky and the Gestapo. It was not Trotsky who had an agreement with Hitler. It was Stalin who signed a Pact with Hitler in August 1939.

It is fitting to end this article by a quote from Leopold Trepper, the leader of the famous anti-Nazi spy network in Western Europe:

> But who did protest at the time? Who rose up to voice his outrage? The Trotskyites can lay claim to this honour. Following the example of their leader, who was rewarded for his obstinacy with the end of an ice-axe, they fought Stalinism to the death, and they were the only ones who did.
>
> Today, the Trotskyites have a right to accuse those who once howled along with the wolves. Let them not forget, however, that they had the enormous advantage over us of having a coherent political system capable of replacing Stalinism. They had something to cling to in the midst of their profound distress at seeing the revolution betrayed. They did not 'confess', for they knew that their confession would serve neither the party nor socialism.

Note

1. The Bolsheviks were members of the Communist Party that gained control of Russia.

The Purge Was an Irrational Result of Stalin's Paranoia

Robert S. Robins and Jerrold M. Post

In the following viewpoint, a political professor and a psychology professor argue that Stalin's paranoia originated in childhood abuse. The authors say that Stalin resented authority because of his father's mistreatment of him. They argue that Stalin was personally cruel and sadistic; he pursued enemies ruthlessly and behaved as a classic paranoid. The authors conclude that Stalin's personal paranoia and pathology were responsible for the murderous violence of the Soviet purges under his reign. Robert S. Robins is a former professor of political science at Tulane University; Jerrold M. Post is a professor of psychiatry, political psychology, and international affairs at George Washington University.

SOURCE. Robert S. Robins and Jerrold M. Post, "Paranoia in Power: Pol Pot, Idi Amin, and Joseph Stalin," *Political Paranoia: The Psychopolitics of Hatred.* New Haven: Yale University Press, 1997, pp. 267–275. Copyright © 1997 by Yale University Press. All rights reserved. Reproduced by permission.

Despite the ruthless practices and policies under [first Soviet ruler Vladimir] Lenin's rule, no one has suggested that Lenin was personally paranoid. Lenin and [Joseph] Stalin did have their similarities. Both, for example, were intolerant of opposition. Their differences, however, were crucial. Lenin dealt with his opposition by expulsion or exile, Stalin by extermination. It was Stalin's consuming desire to murder anyone he suspected was or might become an enemy. He brought the paranoid dynamic into what was already a brutal dictatorship.

Stalin's Childhood

The difficult circumstances of Stalin's childhood and adolescence foreshadowed his harsh rule. Born Iosif Dzhugashvili in 1879 in Georgia, Stalin was descended from illiterate peasants. He barely survived a severe bout of smallpox at age five, and an accidental injury to his left arm in childhood left him with a permanent impairment. It was, however, the beatings Stalin absorbed from his father, a violent man who drank heavily and who beat his wife as well, that hardened Stalin's nature. A boyhood friend, Joseph Iremashvili, described Stalin's travails and their consequences: "Undeserved and severe beatings made the boy as hard and heartless as the father was. Since all people in authority seemed to him to be like his father, there soon arose in him a vengeful feeling against all people in authority standing above him. From childhood on, the realization of his thoughts of revenge became the aim to which everything else was subordinated."

> 'Undeserved and severe beatings made the boy as hard and heartless as the father was.'

Unable to identify the intemperate father's viciousness as the problem, the child who is beaten characteristically develops an inner sense of guilt. One way of defending against this is to develop paranoid mechanisms to project the internal "badness" onto outside persecutors. Another way of mastering the intolerable feelings is to identify with the punitive parent, to do to others as had been done to you. It appears that both projection and identification with the aggressor became core features of Stalin's personality and significantly influenced his political leadership.

According to Iremashvili, when Stalin was in the Gori Church School he became fascinated by Georgian literature and tales of Georgian resistance fighters who fought the invading Russians. He especially liked the story of Koba, depicted in *The Patricide*. Based on a historical episode, this tale describes Koba, a Caucasian Robin Hood who, when not helping the poor, avenges himself upon his enemies. Young Dzhugashvili (who was not to assume the pseudonym Stalin until twenty years later) demanded that everyone call him Koba.

At age seventeen, Stalin left Gori to enter the Russian Orthodox theological seminary in Tbilisi, an environment as brutalizing in its own way as the home he had left. The monks spied on their adolescent charges, eavesdropping and searching through their possessions for such banned items as secular books. This environment heightened Stalin's distaste for religion and authority. His daughter Svetlana wrote of the effects of these experiences: "In a young man who had never for a moment believed in the life of the spirit or in God, endless prayers and enforced religious training could only produce contrary results. . . . From his experiences at the seminary he came to the conclusion that men were intolerant, coarse, deceiving their flocks in order to hold them in obedience; that they intrigued, [and] lied."

These experiences also sharpened Stalin's skills in dissimulation. He learned to conceal his inner rage, rebellion, and wish for revenge behind a facade of calmness and agreement. Stalin's form of rebellion was to steep himself in banned books, particularly the writings of [founder of communism Karl] Marx and Lenin. Just as he hated his father and the monks, he idealized Lenin, calling him a "leader of the highest life, a mountain eagle." Lenin had replaced the "soaring eagle" Koba as Stalin's idealized hero. The eloquence of Lenin's writings on the need to overthrow oppressive authority found fertile ground in young Stalin. Lenin provided an ideological conduit and a political channel for Stalin's vengeful feelings toward authority. According to [historian] Robert Tucker, Lenin's beliefs led Stalin to identify his own enemies as history's.

Stalin as an Early Revolutionary

Stalin left the seminary at age twenty and spent the next ten years as a political organizer and agitator. A coworker described the activist Stalin (then still known as Koba), conveying well his paranoid style: "He treated me suspiciously. After lengthy questioning he handed me a stack of illegal literature . . . He saw me to the door with the same guarded, mistrustful expression. Koba would arrive [late] with a book under his shortened left arm and sit somewhere to the side or in a corner. He would listen in silence until everyone had spoken. He always spoke last. Taking his time, he would compare the different views, weigh all the arguments . . . and make his own motion with great finality, as though concluding the discussion."

Stalin was a leader in the 1901 May Day demonstrations in Tbilisi, in which two thousand workers clashed with the police, and in the labor confrontation in Batum in 1902, in which fifteen striking oil workers were killed by government troops. He was arrested after the Batum confrontation, imprisoned, and sent to exile in Siberia, from which he ultimately escaped to rejoin Lenin in the work of revolution. In an underground press article published in 1905 entitled "The Class of Proletarians and the Party of Proletarians," Stalin emphasized militant aggression and organizational control. The party would

now be a "fortress, the doors of which are only open to the worthy." Stalin was often abrasive in his dealings with other revolutionary leaders; he was quick to take slight, resentful of their superior education and intellectual attainments.

A lasting humiliation to Stalin was his failure to play a leading role in the culminating events of 1917. Indeed, [Leon] Trotsky played a much more consequential role in the seizure of power, second only to Lenin in his importance. When Lenin returned from exile, Stalin's presence was not noted in the records of the meeting in Petrograd. In his official biography, Stalin recast his role, claiming that he rather than Trotsky orchestrated the events, falsely identifying himself as Lenin's equal.

> "Stalin's rivalry with Trotsky was bitter, for Trotsky occupied the position Stalin coveted."

Stalin's rivalry with Trotsky was bitter, for Trotsky occupied the position Stalin coveted. After Lenin's death, Stalin systematically moved to consolidate his control and to rewrite Trotsky's role in the history of the revolution. He characterized Trotsky's "permanent revolution" as the very opposite of Lenin's theory of "proletarian revolution." After Trotsky's forced resignation in 1925, Stalin, characteristically concealing his aggressive, paranoid, controlling nature behind a temperate facade, counseled moderation in responding to those Bolsheviks who disagreed with the preferred party line. The man who was to cut off 40 million heads stated that "cutting off heads is fraught with major dangers for the party." Stalin was not able to heed his own sage warning concerning the dire consequences of "cutting off heads," and, as he noted, once the process was initiated, there was no stopping it. . . .

Stalin's Murders

Stalin killed those who were close to him as well as those he designated as enemies or potential enemies. In the late

Photo on previous page: Joseph Stalin's childhood home, in which he endured abuse at the hands of his father, is housed in a marble monument in his native Georgia. (© Margaret Bourke-White/Time & Life Pictures/Getty Images.)

1930s alone, Stalin killed the chief of the general staff, the chief political commissar of the army, the supreme commanders of all important military districts, 99 percent of all Soviet ambassadors, 98 of 139 members of the Central Committee of the Seventeenth Party Congress, and, eventually, the two chiefs of his secret service, who had been responsible for killing all those just listed.

> Stalin enjoyed inflicting pain upon his foes and would sometimes specify the type of torture to be used on prisoners.

Stalin enjoyed inflicting pain upon his foes and would sometimes specify the type of torture to be used on prisoners. A particular source of pleasure to him was maintaining life-and-death control through random terror. An example of what [philosopher] Erich Fromm has characterized as Stalin's "nonsexual sadism" concerns Sergei Ivanovich Kavtaradze, who had once hidden Stalin from detectives. Stalin rehabilitated the Trotsky-tainted Kavtaradze, who returned the favor by writing an adulatory newspaper article. This was not enough for Stalin, however, and he had Kavtaradze and his wife arrested, tortured, and sentenced to be shot. Kavtaradze, after being kept in his cell for months, was suddenly taken to the office of the chief of the secret police, Lavrenti Beria, where he was reunited with his wife, who seemed to have aged by years. Although the couple was permitted to resume their life, Stalin continued his cat-and-mouse game, having Kavtaradze to dinner and even unexpectedly dropping in for an occasional social call with Beria. At dinner Stalin would play the host, serving his former savior, joking and reminiscing. Yet Stalin's menace would suddenly appear. At one dinner Stalin said to the fearful Kavtaradze, "And still you wanted to kill me."

Stalin would reassure anxious officials that they were in his favor, only to arrest them days later. As Fromm recounts, one evening the wife of a deputy commissar who was hospitalized received an unexpected phone call from Stalin: "'I hear you are going about on foot,' Stalin said. 'That's no good. People might think what they shouldn't. I'll send you a car if yours is being repaired.' And the next morning a car from the Kremlin garage arrived . . . But two days later her husband was arrested right from the hospital."

During the purges Stalin frequently watched the trials from behind a curtain, revealing his presence only by the occasional flare of the matches as he lit and relit his pipe. To oppose Stalin was to ensure lifelong enmity. He never forgot a slight and would often avenge it many years later. Discussing his idea of a perfect day with some comrades, Stalin indicated, "Mine is to plan an artistic revenge upon an enemy, carry it out to perfection, and then go home and go peacefully to bed."

Paranoia

Stalin's pleasure in revenge was not simply an indulgence. It sprang from the relief of eliminating an enemy. Believing he was surrounded by enemies, Stalin was paranoid to the core. One of his principal lieutenants, Nikita Khrushchev, commented, "Sometimes [Stalin] would glare at you and say 'Why don't you look me in the eye today? Why are you averting your eyes from mine?' or some other such stupidity. . . . Stalin had instilled in the consciousness of us all the suspicion that we were surrounded by enemies, that we should try to find an unexposed traitor or saboteur in everyone. Whenever we had a dinner with him, Stalin wouldn't touch a single dish or hors d'oeuvre or bottle until someone else had tested it. This shows he had gone off the deep end." Khrushchev also recalled that, after distributing to his inner circle information about what he called the "doctors' plot," a murderous conspiracy headed

> "Believing he was surrounded by enemies, Stalin was paranoid to the core.

by a cabal of Jewish doctors, Stalin said, "You are blind like young kittens . . . What will happen without me? The country will perish because you do not know how to recognize enemies."

The ruthless rooting out of enemies is the sine qua non [essential quality] of the paranoid despot. In order to survive, a despot must trust no one. But the very action of accusing imagined enemies creates enemies. The severity of Stalin's paranoia left no one free of suspicion, no matter how dedicated and loyal his previous service. According to Stalin's daughter, if Stalin suspected anyone of disloyalty he would try to destroy him, regardless of their previous relationship.

Moreover, Stalin did not have to suspect someone of disloyalty to have him murdered. His fear of betrayal was projective, prospective, and prophylactic. Stalin had many high military officers killed before World War II because he reasoned that it would be in their interest to betray the Soviet Union and cooperate with the far better equipped Germans. He decided to have them killed before the idea occurred to them. Furthermore, the terror of 1934–1939 had no political necessity. The Communists and Stalin were secure by that time. The terror was simply a reflection of Stalin's personal pathology.

How could Stalin, who displayed his paranoia so obviously to intimates, avoid acquiring the reputation of a paranoid? Above all, the events in question took place in an intensely partisan context, and the world had an imperfect idea of what was going on. Another reason concerned Stalin's personality and the paranoid dynamic.

Stalin's favorite image in describing his enemies was that of "masks." Stalin was projecting on others what he himself was doing. Paranoids live in a world in which everyone is in disguise. It is not surprising that they also veil their nature behind a false personality. Stalin did this throughout his life, and it served him well. Unlike [Adolf] Hitler . . . Stalin presented himself to all but his closest intimates as the most moderate of men. He manifested nothing of the paranoid style.

Stalin's Mask

Stalin's own mask was remarkably effective. At Lenin's death the Bolsheviks, still operating within the collegial context that Lenin had fostered, sought a leader who would be "practical and sober minded," someone bland and unexceptional. Many feared that another Napoléon Bonaparte would arise, and they focused their fear on Trotsky, not Stalin. Ironically, Stalin was selected in part because he was seen as an unthreatening, gray bureaucrat.

Not all the Bolsheviks, however, were convinced of Stalin's meekness. Lenin himself, in a final testament, warned against Stalin. Nikolai Bukharin, an intellectual who had spent most of his life outside Russia and who became one of the founders of the Soviet Union, sensed Stalin's inexorable consolidation of power and one-man rule. Desperate, he warned Lev Kamenev, one-time politburo chairman, that Stalin was a "Ghengis Khan [whose] line is ruinous for the whole revolution. . . . He has made concessions only so that he can cut our throats later." In his notes of a meeting with Lenin, Kamenev observed, "Stalin knows only one method: . . . to plant a knife in the back."

> In face-to-face encounters with nonintimates, Stalin wore a mask of reasonableness and moderation, even kindliness.

But for the most part Stalin's disguise was effective. In face-to-face encounters with nonintimates, Stalin wore a mask of reasonableness and moderation, even kindliness. To the observing world, he was genial "Uncle Joe.". . .

Stalin's image was that of a calm and kindly figure, a distant czarlike god. As a Marxist leading a Marxist revolution,[1] Stalin should have found conspiratorial explanations—among the most personal of behaviors—

unattractive. The fact that they so obsessed him points to the crucial role that his personal psychology played in creating the terror.

Note

1. Marxists believed that historical forces and social classes, not individuals, were responsible for historical events.

The Death Tolls of Stalin's Reign Are Underestimated

R.J. Rummel

In the following viewpoint, a political science professor says that Stalin is typically said to have killed 20 million people. The author argues that this figure is far too low, and maintains that in fact Stalin probably was responsible for the deaths of around 43 million people. He says that this is more people than were killed during slavery and comparable to the number of people killed by the Black Death. He says the annual risk of death by the government for those living under Stalin's regime was greater than the chance of dying of cancer or dying in an auto accident is today. The author concludes that not enough people know the scope of Stalin's atrocities. R.J. Rummel is a professor emeritus of political science at the University of Hawaii.

SOURCE. R.J. Rummel, "How Many Did Stalin Really Murder?," *Distributed Republic*, May 1, 2006. Copyright © 2006 by R.J. Rummel. All rights reserved. Reproduced by permission.

May Day [2006] is coming up, which used to be a day of celebration in the Soviet Union with an impressive show of weapons and infinitely long parade of soldiers. Perhaps, then, it would be appropriate to pay special attention on this day to the human cost of communism in this symbolic home of Marxism, and worldwide. This [viewpoint] is on Stalin and the Soviet Union.

More than 20 Million

By far, the consensus figure for those that Joseph Stalin murdered when he ruled the Soviet Union is 20,000,000. You probably have come across this many times. Just to see how numerous this total is, look up "Stalin" and "20 million" in Google, and you will get 183,000 links. Not all settle just on the 20,000,000. Some links will make this the upper and some the lower limit in a range. Yet, virtually no one who uses this estimate has gone to the source, for if they did and knew something about Soviet history, they would realize that the 20,000,000 is a gross under estimate of what is likely the Stalin's true human toll.

> 20,000,000 is a gross under estimate of what is likely Stalin's true human toll.

The figure comes from the book by Robert Conquest, *The Great Terror: Stalin's Purge of the Thirties.* In his appendix on casualty figures, he reviews a number of estimates of those that were killed under Stalin, and calculates that the number of executions from 1936 to 1938 was probably about 1,000,000; that from 1936 to 1950 about 12,000,000 died in the camps; and 3,500,000 died in the 1930–1936 collectivization. Overall, he concludes:

> Thus we get a figure of 20 million dead, which is almost certainly too low and might require an increase of 50 percent or so, as the debit balance of the Stalin regime for twenty-three years.

A man holds a skull fragment in what is believed to be a mass grave of nearly thirty thousand bodies outside St. Petersburg, Russia. Some argue that the number of dead from Stalin's reign is much higher than currently believed. (© AP Images/ Dmitry Lovetsky.)

In all the times I've seen Conquest's 20,000,000 reported, not once do I recall seeing his qualification attached to it.

Considering that Stalin died in 1953, note what Conquest did not include—camp deaths after 1950, and before 1936; executions 1939–53; the vast deportation

ESTIMATED MURDERS BY SOVIET REGIME		
Period	**From (Year)**	**Most Probable Estimate**
Civil War	1917	3,284
NEP	1923	2,200
Collectivization	1929	11,440
Great Terror	1936	4,345
Pre-WWII	1939	5,104
World War II	1941	13,053
Post-War	1946	15,613
Post-Stalin	1954	6,872
Total		**61,911**

Taken from: R.J. Rummel, "Table 1," *Freedom, Democide, War*. www.hawaii.edu.

of the people of captive nations into the camps, and their deaths 1939–1953; the massive deportation within the Soviet Union of minorities 1941–1944; and their deaths; and those the Soviet Red Army and secret police executed throughout Eastern Europe after their conquest during 1944–1945 is omitted. Moreover, omitted is the deadly Ukrainian famine Stalin purposely imposed on the region and that killed 5 million in 1932–1934. So, Conquest's estimates are spotty and incomplete.

I did a comprehensive overview of available estimates, including those by Conquest, and wrote a book, *Lethal Politics,* on Soviet democide [the murder of people by a government] to provide understanding and context for my figures. I calculate that the Communist regime,

1917–1987, murdered about 62,000,000 people, around 55,000,000 of them citizens (for a periodization of the deaths).

Stalin, Slavery, and the Black Death

As for Stalin, when the holes in Conquest's estimates are filled in, I calculate that Stalin murdered about 43,000,000 citizens and foreigners, over twice Conquest's total. Therefore, the usual estimate of 20 million killed in Soviet democide is far off for the Soviet Union per se, and even less than half of the total Stalin alone murdered.

But, these are all statistics and hard to grasp. Compare my total of 62,000,000 for the Soviet Union and 43,000,000 for Stalin to the death from slavery of 37,000,000 during the 16th to the 19th century; or to the death of from 25,000,000 to 75,000,000 in the Black Death (bubonic plague), 1347–1351, that depopulated Europe.

Another way of looking at this is that the annual risk of a person under Soviet control being murdered by the regime was 1 out of 222. But, compare—the annual risk of anyone in the world dying from war was 1 out of 5,556, from smoking a pack of cigarettes a day was 1 out of 278, from any cancer was 1 out of 357, or for an American to die in an auto accident was 1 out of 4,167.

Now, I must ask, with perhaps an unconscious touch of outrage in my voice, why is this death by Marxism, so incredible and significant in its magnitude, unknown or unappreci-

> Why is this death by Marxism, so incredible and significant in its magnitude, unknown or unappreciated?

ated compared to the importance given slavery, cancer deaths, auto accident deaths, and so on? Especially, especially I must add again, when unlike cancer, auto accidents, and smoking, those deaths under Marxism in the Soviet Union were *intentionally* caused? They were murdered.

When you see again the figure of 20,000,000 deaths for Stalin or the Soviet Union, double or triple them in your mind.

The Death Tolls of Stalin's Reign Have Been Overestimated

Timothy Snyder

In the following viewpoint, a historian says that until recently historians thought that Stalin killed more people than Adolf Hitler. They have also thought that Hitler's regime was uniquely motivated by racial hatred. The opening of Soviet archives, however, has revealed that Stalin was responsible for fewer deaths than initially thought—around 6 million rather than 20 million. Thus, Stalin killed less than the 11 million murdered by Hitler. The author notes, however, that records have also shown Stalin was more motivated by ethnic and racial hatred than historians initially believed. Timothy Snyder is a professor of history at Yale University.

SOURCE. Timothy Snyder, "Hitler vs. Stalin: Who Was Worse?," *New York Review of Books* blog, January 27, 2011. www.nybooks.com /blogs/nyrblog. Copyright © 2011 Timothy Snyder. Reproduced by permission. All rights reserved.

As we recall the Red Army's liberation of Auschwitz on January 27, 1945, sixty-six years ago today, we might ask: who was worse, [Adolf] Hitler or [Joseph] Stalin?

The Question of Numbers

In the second half of the twentieth century, Americans were taught to see both Nazi Germany and the Soviet Union as the greatest of evils. Hitler was worse, because his regime propagated the unprecedented horror of the Holocaust, the attempt to eradicate an entire people on racial grounds. Yet Stalin was also worse, because his regime killed far, far more people—tens of millions, it was often claimed—in the endless wastes of the Gulag [the Soviet prison camps]. For decades, and even today, this confidence about the difference between the two regimes—quality versus quantity—has set the ground rules for the politics of memory. Even historians of the Holocaust generally take for granted that Stalin killed more people than Hitler, thus placing themselves under greater pressure to stress the special character of the Holocaust, since this is what made the Nazi regime worse than the Stalinist one. . . .

> We know now that the Germans killed more people than the Soviets did.

Today, after two decades of access to Eastern European archives, and thanks to the work of German, Russian, Israeli, and other scholars, we can resolve the question of numbers. The total number of noncombatants killed by the Germans—about 11 million—is roughly what we had thought. The total number of civilians killed by the Soviets, however, is considerably less than we had believed. We know now that the Germans killed more people than the Soviets did. That said, the issue of quality is more complex than was once thought. Mass murder in the Soviet Union sometimes involved motivations, especially national and ethnic ones, that can be disconcertingly close to Nazi motivations.

It turns out that, with the exception of the war years, a very large majority of people who entered the Gulag left alive. Judging from the Soviet records we now have, the number of people who died in the Gulag between 1933 and 1945, while both Stalin and Hitler were in power, was on the order of a million, perhaps a bit more. The total figure for the entire Stalinist period is likely between two million and three million. The Great Terror and other shooting actions killed no more than a million people, probably a bit less. The largest human catastrophe of Stalinism was the famine of 1930–1933, in which more than five million people starved.

Deliberate Starvation

Of those who starved, the 3.3 million or so inhabitants of Soviet Ukraine who died in 1932 and 1933 were victims of a deliberate killing policy related to nationality. In early 1930, Stalin had announced his intention to "liquidate" prosperous peasants ("kulaks") as a class so that the state could control agriculture and use capital extracted from the countryside to build industry. Tens of thousands of people were shot by Soviet state police and hundreds of thousands deported. Those who remained lost their land and often went hungry as the state requisitioned food for export. The first victims of starvation were the nomads of Soviet Kazakhstan, where about 1.3 million people died. The famine spread to Soviet Russia and peaked in Soviet Ukraine. Stalin requisitioned grain in Soviet Ukraine knowing that such a policy would kill millions. Blaming Ukrainians for the failure of his own policy, he ordered a series of measures—such as sealing the borders of that Soviet republic—that ensured mass death.

> " Blaming Ukrainians for the failure of his own policy, [Stalin] ordered a series of measures . . . that ensured mass death. "

In 2010, Russian president Vladimir Putin (center) attends a memorial for the 1940 massacre of twenty-two thousand Polish officers in the Katyn forest. (© Sasha Mordovets/Getty Images.)

In 1937, as his vision of modernization faltered, Stalin ordered the Great Terror. Because we now have the killing orders and the death quotas, inaccessible so long as the Soviet Union existed,[1] we now know that the number of victims was not in the millions. We also know that, as in the early 1930s, the main victims were the peasants, many of them survivors of hunger and of concentration camps. The highest Soviet authorities ordered 386,798 people shot in the "Kulak Operation" of 1937–1938. The other major "enemies" during these years were people belonging to national minorities who could be associated with states bordering the Soviet Union: some 247,157 Soviet citizens were killed by the NKVD [the Soviet secret police] in ethnic shooting actions.

Ethnic Killing

In the largest of these, the "Polish Operation" that began in August 1937, 111,091 people accused of espionage for Poland were shot. In all, 682,691 people were killed during the Great Terror, to which might be added a few hundred thousand more Soviet citizens shot in smaller actions. The total figure of civilians deliberately killed under Stalinism, around six million, is of course horribly high. But it is far lower than the estimates of twenty million or more made before we had access to Soviet sources. At the same time, we see that the motives of these killing actions were sometimes far more often national, or even ethnic, than we had assumed. Indeed it was Stalin, not Hitler, who initiated the first ethnic killing campaigns in interwar Europe.

> It was Stalin, not Hitler, who initiated the first ethnic killing campaigns in interwar Europe.

Until World War II, Stalin's regime was by far the more murderous of the two. Nazi Germany began to kill on the Soviet scale only after the Molotov-Ribbentrop Pact [a nonaggression pact between Hitler and Stalin] in the summer of 1939 and the joint German-Soviet invasion of Poland that September. About 200,000 Polish civilians were killed between 1939 and 1941, with each regime responsible for about half of those deaths. This figure includes about 50,000 Polish citizens shot by German security police and soldiers in the fall of 1939, the 21,892 Polish citizens shot by the Soviet NKVD in the Katyn massacres of spring 1940, and the 9,817 Polish citizens shot in June 1941 in a hasty NKVD operation after Hitler betrayed Stalin and Germany attacked the USSR. Under cover of the war and the occupation of Poland, the Nazi regime also killed the handicapped and others deemed unfit in a large-scale "euthanasia" program that accounts for 200,000 deaths. It was this policy that brought asphyxiation by carbon monoxide to the fore as a killing technique.

Nazi Killings

Beyond the numbers killed remains the question of intent. Most of the Soviet killing took place in times of peace, and was related more or less distantly to an ideologically-informed vision of modernization. Germany bears the chief responsibility for the war, and killed civilians almost exclusively in connection with the practice of racial imperialism. Germany invaded the Soviet Union with elaborate colonization plans. Thirty million Soviet citizens were to starve, and tens of millions more were to be shot, deported, enslaved, or assimilated. Such plans, though unfulfilled, provided the rationale for the bloodiest occupation in the history of the world. The Germans placed Soviet prisoners of war in starvation camps, where 2.6 million perished from hunger and another half million (disproportionately Soviet Jews) were shot. A million Soviet citizens also starved during the siege of Leningrad. In "reprisals" for partisan action, the Germans killed about 700,000 civilians in grotesque mass executions, most of them Belarusians and Poles. At the war's end the Soviets killed tens of thousands of people in their own "reprisals," especially in the Baltic states, Belarus, and Ukraine. Some 363,000 German soldiers died in Soviet captivity.

Hitler came to power with the intention of eliminating the Jews from Europe; the war in the east showed that this could be achieved by mass killing. Within weeks of the attack by Germany (and its Finnish, Romanian, Hungarian, Italian, and other allies) on the USSR, Germans, with local help, were exterminating entire Jewish communities. By December 1941, when it appears that Hitler communicated his wish that all Jews be murdered, perhaps a million Jews were already dead in the occupied Soviet Union. Most had been shot over pits, but thousands were asphyxiated in gas vans. From 1942, carbon monoxide was used at the death factories Chełmno, Bełżec, Sobibór, and Treblinka to kill Polish and some other European Jews. As the Holocaust spread to the rest of occupied Europe, other Jews were gassed by hydrogen cyanide at Auschwitz-Birkenau.

Overall, the Germans, with much local assistance, deliberately murdered about 5.4 million Jews, roughly 2.6 million by shooting and 2.8 million by gassing (about a million at Auschwitz, 780,863 at Treblinka, 434,508 at Belzec, about 180,000 at Sobibór, 150,000 at Chełmno, 59,000 at Majdanek, and many of the rest in gas vans in occupied Serbia and the occupied Soviet Union). A few hundred thousand more Jews died during deportations to ghettos or of hunger or disease in ghettos. Another 300,000 Jews were murdered by Germany's ally Romania. Most Holocaust victims had been Polish or Soviet citizens before the war (3.2 million and 1 million respectively). The Germans also killed more than a hundred thousand Roma [a European ethnic group, sometimes referred to as gypsies].

All in all, the Germans deliberately killed about 11 million noncombatants, a figure that rises to more than 12 million if foreseeable deaths from deportation, hunger, and sentences in concentration camps are included. For the Soviets during the Stalin period, the analogous figures are approximately six million and nine million. These figures are of course subject to revision, but it is very unlikely that the consensus will change again as radically as it has since the opening of Eastern European archives in the 1990s. Since the Germans killed chiefly in lands that later fell behind the Iron Curtain, access to Eastern European sources has been almost as important to our new understanding of Nazi Germany as it has been to research on the Soviet Union itself. (The Nazi regime killed approximately 165,000 German Jews.)

Note

1. The Soviet Union collapsed in 1991.

Stalin's Atrocities Were as Great as Hitler's

Ron Rosenbaum

In the following viewpoint, a US journalist argues that the West has generally seen Adolf Hitler as more evil than Joseph Stalin. He says that this is in part because the Holocaust is seen as uniquely horrible, and in part because some on the Left want to preserve communism even while rejecting Stalinism. However, the author argues, a fuller knowledge of the Ukrainian famine makes such distinctions impossible. He says that during the Ukrainian famine, in which Stalin deliberately created mass starvation, many were reduced to cannibalism and ate their own children. The author concludes that given such atrocities, there can be no distinction between the evil of Hitler and the evil of Stalin. Ron Rosenbaum is the author of *Explaining Hitler*.

How much should the cannibalism count? How should we factor it into the growing historical-moral-political argument over how to compare

SOURCE. Ron Rosenbaum, "Stalin, Cannibalism, and the True Nature of Evil," *Slate*, February 7, 2011. Copyright © 2011 by Slate. All rights reserved. Reproduced by permission.

[Adolf] Hitler's and [Joseph] Stalin's genocides, and the death tolls of communism and fascism in general. I know I had not considered it. I had really not been aware of the extent of the cannibalism that took place during the Stalinist-enforced famine in the Ukraine in 1933 until I read Yale University history professor Timothy Snyder's shocking, unflinching depiction of it in *Bloodlands*, his groundbreaking new book about Hitler's and Stalin's near-simultaneous genocides.

The Ukraine Death Camp

For the past three decades, beginning with what was called in Germany the *Historikerstreit,* or historians' battle, continuing with the 1997 French publication of *The Black Book of Communism* (which put the death toll from communist regimes at close to 100 million compared with 25 million from Hitler and fascism), there has been a controversy over comparative genocide and comparative evil that has pitted Hitler's mass murders against Stalin's, [China's chairman] Mao's, and [Cambodia's] Pol Pot's.

I had been all too vaguely aware of the role the Stalin-imposed Ukraine famine played in the argument—according to many calculations, it added more than 3 million dead to the sum of Stalin's victims.

But I suppose that, without looking deeply into it, I had considered Stalin's state-created famine a kind of "soft genocide" compared with the industrialized mass murder of Hitler's death camps or even with the millions of victims of Stalin's own purges of the late '30s and the gulags they gave birth to.

Snyder's book, while controversial in some respects, forces us to face the facts about the famine, and the cannibalism helps place the Ukraine famine in the forefront of debate, not as some mere agricultural misfortune, but as one of the 20th century's deliberate mass murders.

Students of comparative evil often point out that Stalin caused a higher death toll than Hitler, even without taking the famine deaths into account; those losses were not treated the same way as his other crimes or as Hitler's killing and gassing in death camps. Shooting or gassing is more direct and immediate than starving a whole nation.

> Stalin in effect turned the entire Ukraine into a death camp, and rather than gassing its people, decreed death by famine.

But Snyder's account of the Ukraine famine persuasively makes the case that Stalin in effect turned the entire Ukraine into a death camp and, rather than gassing its people, decreed death by famine.

Should this be considered a lesser crime because it's less "hands-on"? Here's where the accounts of cannibalism caused me to rethink this question—and to examine the related question of whether one can distinguish degrees of evil in genocides by their methodology.

Communism and Rehabilitation

The argument has been simmering for some time because it has consequences for how we think of events in contemporary history. Nazism, it is generally agreed, cannot be rehabilitated in any way, because it was inextricable from Hitler's crimes, but there are some on the left who believe communism can be rehabilitated despite the crimes of Stalin, and despite new evidence that the tactics of terror were innovations traceable to his predecessor [Vladimir] Lenin.

There are those like the Postmodern sophist Slavoj Žižek who argue that Stalin's crimes were his aberrational distortion of an otherwise admirably utopian Marxist-Leninism whose reputation still deserves respect and maybe a Lacanian[1] tweak in light of the genocidal reality of Marxist/Leninist regimes. But can one really separate an ideology from the genocides repeatedly committed in its name?

In reviewing *Bloodlands* in the *New York Review of Books,* my *Slate* colleague Anne Applebaum observed:

Until recently, it was politically incorrect in the West to admit that we defeated one genocidal dictator with the help of another. Only now . . . has the extent of the Soviet Union's mass murders become better known in the West. In recent years, some in the former Soviet sphere of influence . . . have begun to use the word "genocide" in legal documents to describe the Soviet Union's mass killings too.

> Is it possible—without diminishing Hitler's evil—to argue that Stalin's crimes were by some measures worse?

Are there distinctions to be made between Hitler's and Stalin's genocides? Is it possible—without diminishing Hitler's evil—to argue that Stalin's crimes were by some measures worse? If we're speaking of quantity, Stalin's mass murder death toll may have far exceeded Hitler's, with many putting the figure at 20 million or so, depending on what you count.

But quantity probably shouldn't be the only measure. There is also *intent.* To some, Stalin's murders are not on the same plane (or at the same depth), because he may have believed however dementedly that he was acting in the service of the higher goal of class warfare and the universal aspirations of the oppressed working class. As opposed to Hitler, who killed in the service of a base, indefensible racial hatred.

But on the other hand, one could argue, Hitler too may have believed he was serving an idealistic cause, "purifying" humanity of a "plague bacillus" (his charming term for Jews) like a doctor (he often compared himself to [isolator of tuberculosis, Robert] Koch and [French microbiologist Louis] Pasteur).

Indeed, I'll never forget the moment, which I recount in *Explaining Hitler,* when the great historian H.R. Trevor-Roper leaned toward me over a coffee table in London's Oxford and Cambridge Club after I'd asked him whether he felt Hitler knew what he was doing was wrong. No, Trevor-Roper snapped, "Hitler was convinced of his own rectitude."

Soft on Stalin

I find it hard to understand anyone who wants to argue that the murder of 20 million is "preferable" to anything, but our culture still hasn't assimilated the genocidal equivalence between Stalin and Hitler, because, as Applebaum points out, we used the former to defeat the latter.

Consider the fact that downtown New York is home to a genuinely likable literary bar ironically named "KGB." The KGB, of course, was merely the renamed version of Stalin's NKVD, itself the renamed version of the OGPU, the secret police spearhead of his genocidal policies. And under its own name the KGB was responsible for the continued murder and torture of dissidents and Jews until the Soviet Union fell in 1991 (although of course an ex-KGB man named [Vladimir] Putin is basically running the place now).

> The full evil of Stalin still hasn't sunk in.

You could argue that naming a bar "KGB" is just a kind of Cold War kitsch (though millions of victims might take issue with taking it so lightly). But the fact that you can even make the kitsch argument is a kind of proof of the differential way Soviet and Nazi genocides and their institutions are still treated. Would people seek to hold literary readings at a downtown bar ironically named "Gestapo"?

The full evil of Stalin still hasn't sunk in. I know it to be true intellectually, but our culture has not assimilated the magnitude of his crimes. Which is perhaps why the cannibalism jolted me out of any illusion that meaningful distinctions could be made between Stalin and Hitler.

Perhaps we've failed to assimilate what we've learned about Stalin, Soviet communism, and Mao's communism (50 million may have died in the Great Leap Forward famine and the Cultural Revolution's murders)[2] because for some time the simmering argument had a kind of disreputable side. In the mid-'80s there were German historians such as Jürgen Habermas accusing other German historians such as Ernst Nolte of trying to "normalize" the Nazi regime by playing up its moral equivalence to Stalinist Russia, by suggesting even that Hitler's murderous methods were a *response* to Stalinist terror and genocide, which some saw as an attempt to "excuse" Hitler.

But the disreputable uses to which the argument has been put—normalizing Hitler by focusing on Stalin's crimes—should not blind us to the magnitude and consequences of those crimes.

Eating Children

There is no algorithm for evil, but the case of Stalin's has for a long time weighed more heavily the ideological murders and gulag deaths that began in 1937 and played down the millions who—Snyder argues—were just as deliberately, cold-bloodedly murdered by enforced famine in 1932 and 1933.

Here is where the shock of Snyder's relatively few pages on cannibalism brought the question of degrees of evil alive once again to me. According to Snyder's carefully documented account, it was not uncommon during the Stalin-imposed famine in Soviet Ukraine for parents to cook and eat their children.

The bare statement alone is horrifying even to write.

The back story: While Lenin was content, for a time anyway, to allow the new Soviet Union to develop a "mixed economy" with state-run industry and peasant-owned private farms, Stalin decided to "collectivize" the grain-producing breadbasket that was the Ukraine. His agents seized all land from the peasants, expelling landowners and placing loyal ideologues with little agricultural experience in charge of the newly collectivized farms, which

The Holodomor Memorial in Kiev, Ukraine, is a tribute to the lives lost during the famines caused by the purge. US president George W. Bush (second from left) and his wife, Laura (left), visit the memorial in 2008. (© AP Images/ Gerald Herbert.)

began to fail miserably. And to fulfill Five-Year Plan goals, he seized all the grain and food that was grown in 1932 and 1933 to feed the rest of Russia and raise foreign capital, and in doing so left the entire Ukrainian people with nothing to eat—except, sometimes, themselves.

I've read things *as* horrifying, but never more horrifying than the four pages in Snyder's book devoted to cannibalism. In a way I'd like to warn you not to read it; it is, unfortunately, unforgettable. On the other hand, not to read it is a refusal to be fully aware of what kind of world we live in, what human nature is capable of. The Holocaust taught us much on these questions, but alas, there is more to learn. Maybe it's better to live in denial. Better to think of human history Pollyanna-like, as an evolution upward, although sometimes I feel [Charles] Darwin spoke more truly than he knew when he titled his book *The Descent of Man*. Certainly one's understanding of both Stalinism and human nature will be woefully incomplete until one does read Snyder's pages.

Here is an excerpt:

> In the face of starvation, some families divided, parents turning against children, and children against one another. As the state police, the OGPU, found itself obliged to record, in Soviet Ukraine, "Families kill their weakest members, usually children, and use the meat for eating." Countless parents killed and ate their children and then died of starvation later anyway. One mother cooked her son for herself and her daughter. One 6-year-old girl, saved by other relatives, last saw her father when he was sharpening a knife to slaughter her. Other combinations were, of course, possible. One family killed their daughter-in-law, and fed her head to the pigs, and roasted the rest of her body.

> 'One mother cooked her son for herself and her daughter.'

According to Snyder "at least 2,505 people were sentenced for cannibalism in the years 1932 and 1933 in Ukraine, although the actual number of cases was most certainly greater."

One more horror story. About a group of women who sought to protect children from cannibals by gathering them in an "orphanage" in the Kharkov region:

> One day the children suddenly fell silent, we turned around to see what was happening, and they were eating the smallest child, little Petrus. They were tearing strips from him and eating them. And Petrus was doing the same, he was tearing strips from himself and eating them, he ate as much as he could. The other children put their lips to his wounds and drank his blood. We took the child away from their hungry mouths and we cried.

"And appetite, an universal wolf/ So doubly seconded with will and power/ Must make perforce an universal prey/ And last eat up himself." So Shakespeare wrote, but note that he is speaking not just of the appetite for food, but for power. Stalin was the true cannibal.

How should one react to this? There may only have been a few thousand cases, compared with the millions Stalin starved or murdered, compared with Hitler's slaughters, but there is something in these accounts that forces one to realize there are depths of evil one has not been able to imagine before. Killing another human being, killing millions of human beings. Evil. But forcing parents to cook and eat their children—did one know this was in the repertoire of human behavior? Must we readjust radically downward our vision of human nature? That any human could cause or carry out such acts must mean many are capable of it.

Genocide

The point of the controversy really should be not whether Hitler or Stalin was worse, but that there was more than one of them, more than two of course: There are also Pol Pot [architect of a genocide in Cambodia in the 1970s] and the Rwandan killers [in a genocide in 1994], among others.

Even if those 2,500 arrests for cannibalism were dwarfed by the numbers of those 2 million or more starved to death, they have something unspeakable to say, something almost beyond words. In the light of these reports, can those such as Slavoj Žižek still defend Marxism for its utopian universalism and dismiss the cannibalism as unfortunate unintended consequences of too much zealousness in pursuit of a higher cause? Just a detour on the road to Utopia. Tell us, Mr. Žižek, please. (And by the way, to scorn Postmodern Marxism is not to defend the failings of Postmodern capitalism.)

Should we hold different kinds of genocide differentially evil? One would think brutal direct mass slaughter to be the worst form, but forcing human beings to descend to cannibalizing their children goes beyond physical torture and killing. It is spiritual torture, murder of the souls. In a way more vicious and wicked because the enforced self-degradation is unimaginable in its suffering.

We know what it says about Stalin and his henchmen, all too willing to be accomplices of this horror. But what about the cannibals? How should we regard them? Purely as victims, with no choice? Certainly they must have suffered mentally and spiritually more than we can imagine. But does that mean they didn't have a choice? If we accept they had a choice are we blaming the victims? Or is it clear they were driven insane by starvation—and cannot be held fully culpable by reason of diminished capacity? On the other hand not every family that starved to death turned to cannibalism; were they of stronger moral constitution?

Snyder is very careful about this. He concedes "cannibalism is a taboo of literature as well as life, as communities seek to protect their dignity by suppressing the record of this desperate mode of survival. Ukrainians outside the Soviet Union have treated cannibalism as a source of great shame."

This is an almost too carefully, thus confusingly, worded sentence. It seems as if he's saying that some communities haven't sought to suppress the facts, but feel shame—"Ukrainians outside the Soviet Union." But there is no more Soviet Union. What did or do the Ukrainians who now have their own nation feel? What are they supposed to feel? Victimized into being perpetrators?

These are not easy questions, the ones about how to evaluate degrees of evil. I spend probably too much time thinking about them. Sometimes there are distinctions without a significant difference. Here are some very preliminary thoughts:

—Even if the cannibalism was confined to a few thousand and the larger genocides involved millions, they are not irrelevant to the heart of darkness revealed in the "bloodlands" that lay between Nazi Germany and the Soviet Union.

—There are some distinctions, but no real difference, between Hitler's and Stalin's genocides. Once you get over 5 million, it's fair to say all genocidal monsters are alike.

> The only other conclusion one can draw is that 'European civilization' is an oxymoron.

Finally, the only other conclusion one can draw is that "European civilization" is an oxymoron. These horrors, Nazi and Communist, all arose out of European ideas, political and philosophical, being put into practice. Even the Cambodian genocide had its genesis in the cafes of Paris where Pol Pot got his ideas. Hitler got his ideas in the cafes of Vienna.

"After such knowledge," as [poet T.S.] Eliot said, "what forgiveness?"

Notes

1. Jacques Lacan was a psychoanalyst and philosopher; he is a major influence on Slavoj Žižek.
2. Mao Tse-tung was the Communist leader of China. The Great Leap Forward was Mao's 1958–1961 economic plan for China. The Cultural Revolution was a purge of elements deemed disloyal to Communism in China from 1966–1976.

Stalin Was Not as Evil as Hitler

Avishai Margalit

In the following viewpoint, a philosopher argues that Hitler rejected morality entirely by building his ideology on racism. Thus, Hitler denied the humanity of huge numbers of people. In contrast, the author argues, Stalin's communism imagined a world in which all people would live without scarcity. Thus, he says, Hitler's ideology was itself evil. Stalin's Marxism, on the other hand, accepted morality in theory though it was evil in practice. The author concludes that Nazism was more evil than Stalinism. Avishai Margalit is professor emeritus of philosophy at Hebrew University at Jerusalem and George Kennan Professor at the Institute for Advanced Study in Princeton.

Here is an important distinction between Communism and Nazism. Nazism is an attack on the very idea of morality, whereas Communism,

SOURCE. Avishai Margalit, *The Lesser Evil*, ed. Anthony O'Hear. New York: Cambridge University Press, 2004, pp. 196–201. Copyright © 2004 The Royal Institute of Philosophy and contributors. Reproduced with the permission of Cambridge University Press.

perverse as it was under Stalinism, does not amount to such an attack. The idea is that the main presupposition of morality is shared humanity. Nazi racism both in doctrine and in practice was a conscious attack on the idea of shared humanity, and hence on the very possibility of morality itself. Stalinism was a terrible doctrine, not just an awful practice, but the doctrine did not amount to the very denial of morality. Or so I shall argue.

An Attack on Morality Itself

I borrow from [German philosopher Immanuel] Kant the expression 'radical evil,' though I do not borrow his content. On my account radical evil is any attack on morality itself. By attack I do not mean just a doctrinal nihilistic assault of the idea of morality but an assault by a combination of doctrine and practice. Nazism, in this sense, is radically evil.

Stuart Hampshire [a British philosopher and critic] too regards Nazism as an attack on morality and not just as a gross violation of morality. But Hampshire puts the stress on Nazism's attack on the idea of justice. Understanding justice as the constraints we humans impose on the two human urges—one for domination and the other for a greater share of the rewards for ourselves—then Nazism, in Hampshire's view, is all about unrestricted domination.

> The hard racism of the Nazi variety . . . which calls for eradicating inferior races . . . is a flagrant negation of the idea of shared humanity.

I put the stress on what I regard as the presupposition of morality, namely the idea that all human beings should be subjected to moral treatment solely in virtue of being human. Setting aside 'soft' racism in the sense of trivial racial prejudices, the hard racism of the Nazi variety, namely that which calls for eradicating inferior races such as the Jews and the Gypsies and for enslaving the

Karl Marx on Class Struggle

The history of all hitherto existing society is the history of class struggles.

Freeman and slave, patrician and plebeian, lord and serf, guild-master and journeyman, in a word, oppressor and oppressed, stood in constant opposition to one another, carried on an uninterrupted, now hidden, now open fight, a fight that each time ended, either in a revolutionary reconstitution of society at large, or in the common ruin of the contending classes.

In the earlier epochs of history, we find almost everywhere a complicated arrangement of society into various orders, a manifold gradation of social rank. In ancient Rome we have patricians, knights, plebeians, slaves; in the Middle Ages, feudal lords, vassals, guild-masters, journeymen, apprentices, serfs; in almost all of these classes, again, subordinate gradations.

The modern bourgeois society that has sprouted from the ruins of feudal society has not done away with class antagonisms. It has but established new classes, new conditions of oppression, new forms of struggle in place of the old ones.

Our epoch, the epoch of the bourgeoisie [the capitalist property owner], possesses, however, this distinct feature: it has simplified class antagonisms. Society as a whole is more and more splitting up into two great hostile camps, into two great classes directly facing each other—Bourgeoisie and Proletariat [worker].

SOURCE: *Karl Marx and Friedrich Engels,* The Communist Manifesto, *1848. www.marxist.org.*

Slavs, is a flagrant negation of the idea of shared humanity. Acting on such negation of shared humanity, as the Nazi regime clearly did, is promoting radical evil. It undermines morality itself.

A distinction should be introduced between external evil and internal evil. External evil is radical evil that amounts to a denial of the moral point of view. Internal evil comprises gross violations of morality without denying the idea on which moral judgments are based. The question to be asked in terms of this distinction is, should we exempt Stalinism from the charge of radical evil?

Was Stalinism Radically Evil?

Stalinism professed to be Marxist. Let us take this claim at face value. The problem of denying morality seems already to be a problem for Marxism [or Communism].

Marxism is an ambivalent doctrine about morality. It is motivated by the moral idea of the evil of exploitation. Yet it views morality as an ideology, namely as a set of values and ideas that emerge in particular historical circumstances and function to consolidate the economic and social order of that historical stage. Ideology is most effective in its role of maintaining status quo when it presents itself as the natural order of things, that is, as something that cannot be changed by human action. Both bourgeois [related property owners] economics and bourgeois morality are based on a 'natural' assumption of scarcity; we human beings face, in all societies and in all circumstances, competing demands on scarce resources. The well-known paradox of the diamonds poses this question. Why is the price of diamonds so much higher than the price of water, even though we need water to sustain our life and we can easily do without diamonds? The answer that [Scottish economist] Adam Smith gave is scarcity. In comparison to diamonds there is water in abundance and this explains why water is cheaper than diamonds.

Aristotelians [those who follow the philosophy of Greek thinker Aristotle] such as Maimonides [a Jewish philosopher] thought that scarcity is a fact about the world of matter but not about the world of the spirit. Hence the right way to live is the contemplative life of the spirit. This is exactly the move that Marxist thinking tries to block. Contemplative life is according to Marxism not the only form of life worth living, nor even the preferable one, and it is not the only way to escape scarcity. If paradise is the dream of humanity, as life without scarcity, the Marxists believe that there is no need for such daydreaming. Properly understood, scarcity is an outcome of historical conditions, not of natural conditions. The obstacle of scarcity can be removed in historical times. It can be removed on the one hand by technological innovations that would increase immeasurably what the material world can offer us. And on the other hand it can be removed by creating a classless society with no competing claims on the available resources. This will be done by radically changing people's desires, and hence their patterns of consumption, so much so that the latter will not be governed by scarcity.

> If paradise is the dream of humanity, as life without scarcity, the Marxists believe that there is no need for such daydreaming.

With scarcity gone, economics and morality whither away. In a world without scarcity there is no need for morality any more than there was need for Adam and Eve in paradise to eat from the tree of knowledge so as to know good from evil. Abundance undermines the need for the distinction between good and evil.

Scarcity and Morality

We may very well think that this communist utopia of overcoming scarcity is no more realistic than trying to secure a place in the biblical paradise. But the question is whether the idea of overcoming scarcity, and hence undercutting morality, falls under the heading of undermining morality itself and thus counting as a radical evil.

Some argue that the Nazi genocide, from which these prisoners where rescued, was more evil than that of Joseph Stalin's. (© Margaret Bourke-White/Getty Images.)

My answer: not in the least. After all, in religions that entertain the idea of paradise there are movements that view paradise in antinomian [the idea that faith, not the moral law, is necessary for salvation] terms. Paradise is a place free from religious laws. This does not mean that those movements do not take the religious laws seriously in this world. The mere fact that Communism aspires to overcome morality by creating such conditions that there is no need for it does not undermine morality any more than the aspiration to create situation of perfect health undermines medicine.

But this of course is far from being the whole story about the relation between Communism and ethics, not to say Communism in its Leninist [related to Vladimir Lenin, the first Soviet leader] form. Attached to the idea of bringing about a classless world with no need for morality is the idea that there should be no moral constraints on the project of bringing about such a world. So the situation we are facing is not that of morality now, paradise later. Instead, it is hell now for paradise later: such a great end surely justifies all means. The cliché 'the end justifies the means' is meant to tell this story of ignoring morality in the name of a future without scarcity. So there is no morality at the end, but also no morality on the way. If this is no negation of morality, what is?

Sidney Morgenbesser [a US philosopher] once questioned the cliché by asking jokingly what else should justify the means if not the end. Well, there should be something else on the road to bringing about the end: there should be what [US political philosopher Robert] Nozick calls 'side constraints.' Stalinism is a glaring case of disregard of any moral side constraints in bringing about the desired end. But then the claim is that the way to understand Stalinism morally is not by deontic [ethical rules] side constraints but as a huge exercise in Pascal's wager.[1] A socialist world without scarcity in the future has an infinite utility. The overwhelming expected utility of the future world justifies, on utilitarian grounds, any amount of suffering today. The infinite future bliss dwarfs the suffering of today on an expected utility ground. This Pascalian wager, namely betting on future history, is a bad argument, since if you pump infinite utility into future socialism or into kingdom come then anything goes. Every state of affairs has a tiny probability of bringing about the blissful future: multiply it by the infinite utility of the future and you get an infinite expected utility that justifies that particular state of affairs. In short, the Stalinist use of Pascal's wager can justify fascism as it can justify communism. It can justify everything and hence it justifies nothing.

But with all this moral sophistry about the blissful future, there are of course questions about the road, whether it leads at all to the Promised Land. Or, to switch to a more familiar metaphor, the question is besides breaking eggs Stalinism can produce an omelette. Put literally, were the means taken by Stalinism instrumentally adequate to bringing about the end?

If the end is a world without scarcity then the answer should be a resounding no. But if the end was to create industrial society that could stand up to enemies such as Nazi Germany, then the answers is yes. Awful as these means were, the outcome of WWII shows that they were indeed adequate for that goal. But this gambit of shifting the goal, at least temporarily, from socialism to industrialization is, morally speaking, a red herring. It was used by Stalinist apologetics to justify Stalin's choice of the right method to overcome Nazism. As if Communism was born to combat Nazism, and as if there was no pact between Stalin and Hitler, a pact that Stalin was determined to keep.[2] It is a case of shooting first and drawing the bull's eye later.

> The practice of Stalinism was hellish but its ideals were moral. With Hitlerism both the practice and the ideals were fiendish.

In the Name of Future Humanity

The practice of Stalinism was hellish but its ideals were moral. With Hitlerism both the practice and the ideals were fiendish. So much worse, you might say, for Stalinism. It is much worse to act immorally in the name of moral ideals, just as it is worse to be a hypocrite and act immorally than to act immorally without being hypocritical about it. The Nazis at least did not pretend to behave morally.

I disagree. The cliché that hypocrisy is the homage paid by vice to virtue has, I believe, a profound meaning. Hypocrisy, irritating as it is, at least recognizes morality; and Communism, even in its wretched Stalinist form, is not nihilism. Nazism, unlike Communism in general and Stalinism in particular, is a denial of shared humanity. This is my claim. But is it true?

In a chapter entitled 'The Attack on Humanity' Jonathan Glover rightly points out that Nazi practices carried dehumanization to relentless extremes. But my point is that not only the practice but also the doctrine was one of denying what Raimond Gaita [a German-Australian philosopher] calls 'common humanity,' and I call shared humanity. But then the question is, is it true that the Nazi ideology, confused and confusing as it was, denied the idea of shared humanity? After all, Glover uses as a motto for one of his chapters Hitler's saying, 'Those who see in National Socialism nothing more than a political movement, know scarcely anything of it. It is more even than a religion: it is the will to create mankind anew.' One may cogently argue that this idea would not be alien to Stalin, let alone to Mao [Tsetung, a Chinese Communist leader]. They all talked and acted in the name of a future humanity that they were going to create; none of them was committed to a shared concrete humanity. So why does it matter if you are excluded from future humanity for being a parasitic bourgeois, as in Stalinism, or for being a parasitic Jew, as in Nazism? After all, both categories of human beings, bourgeois and Jews, were perceived in equally inhuman terms—'parasites.'

The idea of future humanity and the idea of shaping 'a new man' are fantasy of many ideologies. Moreover, the idea that there is a class of people that anticipate the future man and the future humanity, be these people 'the workers,' 'the bureaucrats,' or 'the students,' is also an idea shared by many radical ideologies. With it also goes the idea that the humanity of today is, in biblical terms, a 'desert generation' bound to perish on the way to the Promised Land. Stalinism, I maintain, is an extreme case of this dangerous fantasy of callousness towards concrete people in the name of abstract future humanity.

But Hitlerism is something very different. It is the dismembering of humanity into races. It thereby excludes, as a matter of doctrine, groups of people from being deserving of moral consideration of whatever sort. If the Slavs are destined in Hitler's 'future humanity' to be slaves, the ontological [existential] and moral status of the Slavs is no better than that of domestic animals.

When it comes to Nazism there is no room for morality. At most we can find in Nazism perverse hygiene, run by the category of filth. Filth is regarded as a degenerative disease and thereby the degeneration of the master race. Future humanity in Hitler's fantasy is no humanity. It is the master race that replaces the idea of humanity. This is radical evil if anything is. So on my account [British prime minister Winston] Churchill was right in preferring the devil to Hitler.

Notes

1. Pascal's wager says that a person gains heaven if he believes in God if God exists, and loses nothing if God does not exist. Therefore, a rational person should believe in God.
2. In 1939, Stalin and Hitler signed a nonaggression pact, which Hitler later broke.

Stalin Remains Popular in Russia Today

Adrian Blomfield

In the following viewpoint, a journalist reports that Joseph Stalin is growing in popularity in Russia. Polls suggest that Stalin is considered to be a great leader by many Russians. The author says that support for Stalin mostly comes from aging Communists, but even younger people in Russia praise Stalin for industrializing the Soviet Union and defeating the Nazis. The author believes that the Russian government is working to rehabilitate Stalin's image in order to make authoritarian rule seem more acceptable. Adrian Blomfield is the Moscow correspondent for the *Telegraph*.

A couple of years ago I was in the Battle of Stalingrad Museum in the city now known as Volgograd [formerly Stalingrad].

The Greatest Russian Leader?

On the wall of museum director Boris Usik's office hung two paintings, one a delicate watercolour of the late Queen Mother, the other a heroic depiction of Josef Stalin in oils.

Seeing the old tyrant hung so prominently in a state official's office was unnerving at the time. While the odd statue of Stalin had been restored in a couple of village squares, the man who subjected Russia to 31 years of terror had largely disappeared from public view.

> Seeing the old tyrant hung so prominently in a state official's office was unnerving.

Yet over the past couple of years it has once again become cool to revere Stalin, and so it was not much of a surprise to learn that the dictator responsible for perhaps 20 million deaths was leading early voting in a nationwide poll to decide the country's greatest historical figure.

Even during his lifetime, Stalin enjoyed more public support in Russia than many in the West realise. After all, those who opposed him were dispatched to the gulags [prison camps] or their deaths. Others were terrified into silence.

But then, as now, a sizeable chunk of the population either swallowed the propaganda or genuinely believed that Stalin had reinvigorated a moribund nation, turning [it into] a great power while simultaneously saving Europe from [Adolf] Hitler.

For old Communists like Mr Usik, Stalin's name is synonymous with stability in a country that has not had much of it of late. What has struck me, however, is Stalin's cross-generational appeal. I've even heard bright young students praise his disastrous agricultural collectivization [in which private farms were nationalized] policies. Most Russians, even his supporters, acknowledge that Stalin had an awful lot of blood on his hands.

But they argue that it was a period in history when Russia needed a tough man at the top. And they argue that there is much more on the positive side of Stalin's ledger, particularly in the Great Patriotic War [World War II].

While the Soviet Union's role is often minimized in the West, many Russians are unaware of the role played by Britain and the United States in defeating Hitler. They believe the Second World War only began in 1941 and maintain that Russia fought alone for three years until Britain and the United States reluctantly joined the war during the D-Day landings of 1944.

Rehabilitating Stalin

Yet the fact that Stalin's popularity has also grown in recent years—something attested to in opinion polls—is

A bus in St. Petersburg, Russia, is decorated with a portrait of Joseph Stalin in honor of WWII Victory Day celebrations in 2010. (© **AP Images/ Dmitry Lovetsky.**)

undoubtedly partly to do with an unofficial state campaign to rehabilitate his image.

A series of television documentaries, films and books released in recent years have proved little less than eulogies. Then the Kremlin [the Russian government] began to attack the publishing industry for being beholden to Western grants.

> A new history guidebook for teachers . . . glossed over Stalin's crimes and ultimately declared him Russia's greatest leader of the 20th century.

Television news programmes, whose content is dictated by the State, regularly reported that the history text books used in schools had been distorted by the West to skew the representation of Russia's Communist past.

So a new history guidebook for teachers was published last year [2007] which glossed over Stalin's crimes and ultimately declared him Russia's greatest leader of the 20th century.

Despite earlier denials that anything of the sort was planned, the work was republished as a children's text book and while it has not become a mandatory set text most schools know they risk trouble if they try to teach from anything else.

Why is the Kremlin so intent on rehabilitating Stalin? Garry Kasparov, the former chess giant and opposition leader, reckons that by hamming up Stalin's greatness, Russians will be more inclined to forgive the government's march towards authoritarianism.

After all, as the old dictum states, he who controls the present controls the past and he who controls the past controls the future.

Stalin Is Not Popular in Russia Today

Thomas Sherlock

In the following viewpoint, a political science professor argues that Russians do not have a positive opinion of Stalin. This is especially true of younger Russians. He argues that Russians do have some nostalgia for the Soviet system, which was stable and made Russia a world power, as opposed to the recent Russian Republic, which has been chaotic and economically weak. However, he says, this nostalgia does not translate into a desire to return to Soviet times. In addition, the author argues, the Russian government is currently trying to create a better relationship with the West. He says the government knows that praising Stalin interferes with this goal. Thomas Sherlock is a professor of political science at the United States Military Academy at West Point.

SOURCE. Thomas Sherlock, "Confronting the Stalinist Past: The Politics of Memory in Russia," *Washington Quarterly*, vol. 34, no. 2, Spring 2011, pp. 100–103. Copyright © 2011 by Taylor and Francis Group Ltd. All rights reserved. Reproduced by permission.

Assessing the results of their important surveys on Russian political attitudes in early 2006, scholars Sarah Mendelson and Theodore Gerber found significant support overall in Russia for a positive image of Stalin, a phenomenon which they trace in large part to the propaganda machine of the [Vladimir] Putin presidency [of the 2000s]. More recently, in early 2008, Mendelson and Gerber wrote that under Putin, the Kremlin [a term used to denote the Russian government] had launched a campaign to cultivate anti-Westernism as well as nostalgia for the Soviet era, and that these efforts were particularly successful in targeting Russia's youth. Despite these findings, it is possible to draw different conclusions from Russian polls which underline the complexity of Russian attitudes about the Soviet past.

Little Nostalgia for Stalin

How strong is nostalgia for the Soviet Union and do Russia's youth prefer Soviet times to contemporary life? For the overwhelming majority, the answer seems to be "no." A poll in 2010 by VCIOM, the Russian public-opinion firm, revealed that only 7 percent of the 18–24 age group (a core component of the "Putin Generation") fully agreed with the statement that "it would be better if everything was as before *perestroika*" (i.e., during the Brezhnev years).[1] When asked directly which era they would prefer to live in, only four percent of total respondents chose the Stalinist period (only three percent of the 18–24 group). Compared to other segments, the 18–24 group was the least interested in the Soviet era.

Russian attitudes toward Stalin the dictator remain complex. In December 2009, VCIOM released data on how Russians assess Stalin and Stalinism. Reflecting the findings of Mendelson and Gerber, VCIOM reports that Russians have positive feelings toward Stalin more often than negative ones (37 percent versus 24 percent).

Photo on following page: Some critics argue that the negative effects of Stalin's stifling of political opposition continue to be felt in Russia. In 2011, protesters rally in Moscow's Red Square against alleged vote rigging. (© AP Images/Alexander Zemlianichenko.)

Russia Since Stalin

Joseph Stalin died in 1953. He was succeeded by Nikita Khrushchev, who publicly denounced Stalin's policy of repression in a speech in 1956. Khrushchev did not make the Soviet Union a democracy, and, indeed, in 1956 he brutally suppressed a democratic revolution in Hungary. However, the Soviet Union would never again use terror as it had during Stalin's purges.

Khrushchev was displaced in 1964 by Leonid Brezhnev, who reigned for eighteen years, and was followed by a series of other leaders. All continued authoritarian rule, including control of satellite nations in Eastern Europe, such as Poland and East Germany. They all also pursued a policy of animosity to the West that stopped short of open hostilities—a Cold War.

Mikhail Gorbachev came to power in 1985. The Soviet Union was becoming increasingly strained by its large military buildup. Furthermore, Gorbachev, like many of his people, believed in democracy and openness. He allowed people to criticize the government, and he began to allow more freedom in Eastern

Yet Valery Fyodorov, the director of VCIOM, points out that "the overbalance" is due to the "elder generations," with older Russians much more likely to feel respect for Stalin than young Russians (35 percent versus 22 percent). According to other recent polls, 30 percent of older Russians believe that when Stalin died the country lost a "great leader and teacher," while only nine percent of younger Russians share this opinion. Equally important, the 2009 VCIOM poll found that 38 percent of the young generation registered "indifference" to the image of Stalin. Lev Gudkov, the director of the Levada Center, a well-regarded polling organization, found that the number of Russians overall who are indifferent to Stalin has risen over the past eight years from 17 percent to 47 percent. According to the Center's data, the figure for young Russians was approximately 50 percent.

Europe as well. Gorbachev hoped that his reforms would allow the Communist government to renew itself.

Instead, in 1990 and 1991, the Marxist system unraveled. Russia's Eastern European satellites were given independence. Many parts of the Soviet Union, such as Ukraine and Georgia, also became independent states. Russia chose to become a capitalist society headed by President Boris Yeltsin.

Hopes were high in Russia and outside it that the country would become a strong, prosperous democracy. Instead, Russia continued to suffer serious eco-nomic problems. These were in part exacerbated by the swift transition to capitalism, which encouraged corruption as state assets were sold off. In 2000, Vladimir Putin, a former KGB officer, succeeded to the presidency. By most accounts, Putin's government was authoritarian, and freedom and democracy were scaled back. Putin and his ally, Dmitry Medvedev, have continued in power in Russia as of this writing, despite large-scale protests against their leadership in late 2011.

This increasing lack of interest in Stalin seems to challenge the position that pro-Stalinist and pro-Soviet propaganda has significantly shaped Russian public consciousness. Instead, it seems that Putin's efforts to avoid painful historical issues during most of his presidency, coupled with the growth of diverse sources of historical information, has helped produce ambivalence and indifference toward Stalin, not support. While not as dangerous as a long-term pro-Stalin campaign, the Kremlin's approach has left the current generation largely uneducated about Russia's difficult past and potentially adrift morally. For this reason, [Russian President Dmitry] Medvedev recently deplored the lack of knowledge and interest of Russia's youth in the Stalinist purges of the 1930s.

> Medvedev recently deplored the lack of knowledge and interest of Russia's youth in the Stalinist purges of the 1930s.

A Cruel and Inhuman Tyrant

Although disinterest in Stalin and Stalinism is widespread among Russia's youth, polls administered over the last 10 years show that other age groups have strongly negative opinions about the leader and his system. In VCIOM surveys, Russians were asked whether they agreed with the following statement: "Stalin was a cruel and inhuman tyrant who was responsible for the death of millions of people." In 1998, 28 percent of total respondents replied in the affirmative. By 2009, this number had risen to 35 percent. Looking at the issue somewhat differently, another survey asked whether the "repressions of those years were a correct and necessary step of the Soviet regime." The Kremlin-sponsored [Alexander] Filippov handbook [distributed to teachers] of 2007 essentially makes this argument. But in the survey, only two percent of the respondents agreed with the statement. Answering a question about who was responsible for the repressions spanning the 1930s to the early 1950s, 79 percent of the respondents blamed Stalin, the state system, or the state system and Stalin together. Only six percent of the respondents chose to absolve Stalin by answering "neither/someone else/enemies of our country."

It is often suggested that the regret felt by a majority of Russians for the collapse of the Soviet Union is convincing evidence of an effective pro-Soviet propaganda campaign. Indeed, Putin in 2005 had famously called the Soviet demise "the greatest geopolitical catastrophe of the twentieth century." Yet, it should be recalled that popular regret for the Soviet collapse was already commonplace when Putin took office. And although polls in 2000, the year Putin assumed the presidency, showed that 75 percent of the respondents lamented the disintegration of the Soviet Union, surveys conducted by the Levada Center from 1992–2009 demonstrate that feelings of regret among the Russian population (as a whole) had declined to 60 percent by 2009.

An important part of the explanation for this lingering sentiment is the experience of most Russians in the first post-Soviet decade. Rejecting the Soviet past at first seemed acceptable to many Russians in 1990 and 1991, in part because of the widespread—almost euphoric—expectation that the collapse of the Soviet Union would enable Russia to quickly join the ranks of the prosperous and democratic powers. Indeed, the Soviet Union collapsed in large part because foreign models of socioeconomic and political development had become increasingly legitimate, while the Soviet model was rapidly de-sanctified in the eyes of multiple Soviet audiences. Western models of democracy and economic development served as a functional substitute for national historical myths, providing a vision of a stable, just, and affluent society. In this sense, many Russians rejected the Soviet past because they felt it was no longer relevant to their present or future.

Russia's Hardships

The harsh reality of life in the new Russian Republic overturned this assumption. The severe political disorder and economic decline of the 1990s gradually stripped Russians of their belief that a prosperous and democratic Russia would emerge in the near future. In this context, the Soviet past was increasingly reassessed in positive terms, either as a re-legitimated model for social and political development or as an historical frame with the capacity to

> 'Those who do not regret the collapse of the Soviet Union have no heart,' but those who want it to be restored 'have no brain.'

stimulate pride and reinforce individual and group identity, particularly in memories of the extraordinary Soviet sacrifice and victory in World War II.

Yet, it is likely that many Russians who feel this way also share Putin's view that "those who do not regret the collapse of the Soviet Union have no heart," but those who want it to be restored "have no brain." Even Filippov's controversial 2007 handbook portrayed the Soviet Union in the post-Stalin era as dysfunctional and corrupt, and the Soviet collapse in 1991 as largely the result of the system's inability to address burgeoning domestic and foreign problems.

Such attitudes and assessments reflect the general belief that the Soviet system was ultimately a failure even though the era is still valued because it provided the institutional frame for the personal lives of generations. Russia's elites also understand that a project to restore the institutions and ideology of the Soviet Union is beyond their capacity and would in any case be anathema because it would challenge their personal freedom and privileged position in Russia's system of state capitalism. And with its current efforts to forge better relations with the West, Russia's leadership increasingly sees the Stalinist period not as a symbolic resource but as a political liability.

Note

1. *Perestroika* was a restructuring of the Soviet Union to allow more political openness. It occurred under the direction of Mikhail Gorbachev, after the reign of Leonid Brezhnev.

CHAPTER 3

Personal Narratives

Recalling Stalin's Soviet Russia

Owen Matthews

Owen Matthews is the author of Stalin's Children. *In the following viewpoint, Matthews recounts the experiences of Alexander Solzhenitsyn within Stalin's gulags (labor camps). Matthews praises Solzhenitsyn for speaking out and giving a voice to those that Stalin had silenced—including Matthews's own grandfather. Solzhenitsyn became a hero and advocate for those who had suffered in the gulags of Stalin's Russia.*

The truth that Alexander Solzhenitsyn told helped to make Russia free. Mikhail Gorbachev, the last Soviet leader, acknowledged a day after Solzhenitsyn's death at age 89 that the Nobel Prize-winning author and dissident had "helped people see the real nature of

SOURCE. Owen Matthews, "Solzhenitsyn: My Murdered Grandfather's Voice," *Newsweek*, August 4, 2008. Copyright © 2008 by Daily Beast Newsweek. All rights reserved. Reproduced by permission.

the regime"—and that his writings had helped to "make our country free and democratic." At a time when the Soviet system seemed impenetrable and frozen in place forever, Solzhenitsyn brought the terrible reality of the Gulag home not just to foreigners but to ordinary Russians too; in the bright, sanitized world of Soviet propaganda, Solzhenitsyn's writing held a mirror to the Soviet Union's darkest secrets. The State had tried to airbrush the Gulags, the Purges and the famines made by Stalin out of history. Solzhenitsyn spoke for the millions whose voices Stalin had silenced.

> Solzhenitsyn brought the terrible reality of the Gulag home not just to foreigners but to ordinary Russians too.

One of them was my grandfather, Boris Lvovich Bibikov, my mother's father. An enthusiastic Bolshevik, Bibikov had received the Order of Lenin for his part in building the Kharkov Tractor Factory, one of the giant projects of Stalin's industrialization drive of the early 1930s. But in the great Purge of 1937, which Stalin launched against his opponents in the Party, real and imagined, Bibikov found himself accused of crimes against the revolution. He was tried by a secret court on evidence obtained under torture and sentenced to death. The usual method was "nine grams"—the weight of a pistol bullet—to the back of the head. His wife, my grandmother, was sent to the Gulag for fifteen years as the wife of an "enemy of the people" and his two daughters, my mother and aunt, were dispatched to an orphanage for re-education.

Some years ago I was given permission to read my grandfather's secret police file. It contained about three pounds of paper, the sheets carefully numbered and bound, with my grandfather's name entered on the crumbling brown cover in curiously elaborate, copperplate script. The file sat heavily in my lap, eerily malignant, a swollen tumor of paper, and since the careful

bureaucrats who compiled the file neglected to say where he was buried, this stack of paper is the closest thing to Boris Bibikov's earthly remains. For the days that I sat in the former KGB headquarters in Kiev examining the file, Alexander [Ponomarev], a young officer of the Ukrainian Security Service sat with me, reading out passages of barely legible cursive script and explaining legal terms. "Your grandfather believed," said [Ponomarev]. "But do you not think that his accusers believed also? Or the men who shot him?"

Solzhenitsyn once posed the same, terrible question. "If my life had turned out differently, might I myself not have become just such an executioner?" he wrote in *The Gulag Archipelago*, his epic "literary investigation" of Stalin's terror. "If only it was so simple! If only there were evil people somewhere insidiously committing evil deeds, and it were necessary only to separate them from the rest of us and destroy them. But the line dividing good from evil cuts through the heart of every human being. And who is willing to destroy a piece of their own heart?"

Speaking Out

All his life Solzhenitsyn was moved by a powerful, almost mystical, moral sense. He felt compelled to speak out against what he felt was wrong, regardless of the consequences—which in his case were eight years in the Gulag, decades of harassment and denunciation by the Soviet authorities and the craven "intellectuals" who served the regime, and finally twenty years of exile from the country which he loved with a passion.

His first crime against the system was to criticize Stalin in a private letter to a friend in 1945. When the military censor reported the letter to the secret police, Solzhenitsyn, then a young artillery captain twice decorated for valor, was given a perfunctory trial and sent to Stalin's nightmarish Gulags. Like 18 million of his fellow

Photo on previous page: A Russian woman and her son search for food during the famine in 1934. Stalin's policies are blamed for massive "man-made" famines that starved millions of people. (© **London Express/Getty Images.**)

countrymen, he found himself plunged into a parallel world of unimaginable brutality, where prisoners slaved in the Siberian cold on madly futile projects like canals that no one needed and train lines to nowhere. Solzhenitsyn called it the Gulag Archipelago—like islands in a sea of frozen steppe, the Gulags were a state within the state. After his release he penned a short story which described, in simple but devastatingly telling detail, one day in the life of a Gulag inmate named Ivan Denisovich. When it was published in Moscow in 1962 during a brief post-Stalin thaw, Ivan Denisovich caused a sensation.

> Solzhenitsyn's persecutors . . . were often driven by the same motivations as their victims.

Solzhenitsyn's persecutors, like my grandfather's, were often driven by the same motivations as their victims. When people become the building-blocks of history, intelligent men can abdicate moral responsibility. Indeed the Purge—in Russian, "chistka" or "cleaning" —was something heroic to those who made it, just as the building of the great factory was heroic to Bibikov. The difference was that my grandfather made his personal Revolution in physical bricks and concrete, whereas the Secret Police's bricks were class enemies, every one sent to the execution chamber another building-block in the great edifice of socialism.

The men drawn to serve in the Soviet secret police, in the famous phrase of its founder Felix Dzerzhinsky, could either be saints or scoundrels—and clearly the service attracted more than its fair share of sadists and psychopaths. But they were not aliens, not foreigners, but men, Russian men, made of the same tissue and fed by the same blood as their victims. "Where did this wolf-tribe appear from among our own people?" asked Solzhenitsyn. "Does it really stem from our own roots? Our own blood? It is ours."

This was the true, dark genius behind Stalinism—a genius that Solzhenitsyn describes in devastating detail. Not simply to put two strangers into a room, one a victim, one an executioner, and convince the one to kill the other, but to convince both that this murder served some higher purpose. This can happen only when a man becomes a political commodity, a unit in a cold calculation, his life and death to be planned and disposed of just like a ton of steel or a truckload of bricks.

Yet Solzhenitsyn's moral compass, so steady in the black-and-white world of Stalin's Russia, began to waver after the collapse of Communism. He returned to Russia in 1994 after two decades in exile in America and was feted as a nearly messianic figure. But Solzhenitsyn had no love for capitalist Russia and refused to accept a State prize from Boris Yeltsin because he had brought "so much suffering on the Russian people." And when Vladimir Putin—a former KGB officer—began to prune away the anarchic freedoms which Yeltsin had won, Solzhenitsyn hailed his "strong leadership" and brushed aside Putin's KGB past, saying that "every country needs an intelligence service." Yesterday Putin returned the compliment, lamenting Solzhenitsyn's passing as a "heavy loss for Russia." Both Putin and Russia's new president Dmitry Medvedev are expected to attend Solzhenitsyn's funeral at Moscow's Donskoi Monastery on Wednesday [August 6, 2008].

The strangeness of a former KGB officer paying tribute to Russia's greatest dissident is a reflection of just how conflicted Russia remains about its recent past—and in particular the legacy of Stalin. He was the

> [Stalin] was the greatest mass murderer of the last century.

greatest mass murderer of the last century, starving millions in man-made famines and creating a prison system which claimed more lives than the Nazi death camps. Yet recent polls have shown that Stalin is one of Russians' most respected historical figures, and, with the Kremlin's blessing, school history books are being revised to show the "Great Leader" in a more positive light. And Putin described the fall of the Soviet Union as "the greatest geopolitical tragedy of the century." Solzhenitsyn, for all his cordial relations with Putin, could not have disagreed more strongly.

For decades, the Soviet Communist Party claimed to be the "mind, honor and conscience of the people." But the truth was that the Party was the agent of unimaginable human suffering, lies and deception. The true conscience of Russia was Alexander Solzhenitsyn—the man who dared to speak out against the regime and chronicled its crimes in painstaking detail. And in insisting that the Russian people "live not by lies," Solzhenitsyn made a tiny but deep fissure in the wall of hypocrisy which in time was, in time, to crack the whole rotten system apart.

Yet for all his greatness and importance in bringing down the Soviet Union, Solzhenitsyn had become an irrelevance to the thrusting, new, oil-rich Russia of Vladimir Putin. In that lies a tragedy, because Russia has swung back from its infatuation with wild capitalism into what has proved to be a deeper longing for authority and order. Solzhenitsyn, once an idealistic Communist, understood better than most how power can pervert men and ideas. He saw himself as a prophet not just for Russia but for all mankind, and in his later years turned to denouncing the corruptions of capitalism and the dangers of liberalism. But for all his unfashionable conservatism, he believed adamantly in the value of human dignity—and that a State abdicated all moral authority to order society if it abused its citizens. Russia, for all its wealth, remains mired in corruption and injustice. With Solzhenitsyn's death it has lost its conscience, and is a poorer place for it.

A Russian Remembers Childhood During Stalin's Terror

Nina Markovna

Nina Markovna grew up during the 1930s in Russia. In the following viewpoint, she remembers the Stalinist terror and her fears that her father would be seized and imprisoned by the Soviet police. She says that there were many young children whose parents were imprisoned by the Soviets and who were reduced to living in the forest without support. She says that charities and individuals were not allowed by the authorities to help these children. As a result, she remembers, the children took to crime, prostitution, and begging. Markovna recalls that she was terrified of becoming like them if her father was taken away.

SOURCE. From the book *Nina's Journey: A Memoir of Stalin's Russia and the Second World War* by Nina Markovna. Copyright © 1989. Published by Regnery Publishing, Inc. All rights reserved. Reprinted by special permission of Regnery Publishing, Inc., Washington, DC.

Midnight arrived. Slava and I, our stamina exhausted, had moved earlier from the kitchen table to our beds, dozing, yet ears still alert. And then we heard it—crunching in the snow, hurrying steps, steps that sent our blankets onto the floor and us back to the kitchen table. Father cleared away the pile of papers he was working on, papers connected with his bookkeeping that he often had to bring home in order to catch up with an overload of work. The samovar was still warm to the touch, so Mother could have a cup of decent-tasting tea after that long walk. Tea with what? Honey cookies, perhaps, or sugar cookies, or a gorgeous candy, maybe, with strawberry flavoring?

A Car in the Night

Mother tried to come in quietly, not wishing to awaken us if we were asleep, but seeing our not-at-all sleepy eyes riveted on her with a beaming question mark, she all at once began to empty her pockets.

"Ho! Ho! Ho!" she mocked in a masculine voice, imitating Father Frost. "I am loaded with sweets! Look!" And hard sugar candies began to fall out of her mittens like marbles out of a sack. She reached behind the collar of her loose, full blouse and produced several cookies.

To my delight, honey cookies—my favorite—appeared out of Mother's bosom. She reached into her snow boot and produced a pack of cigarettes called *Kasbek*, one of the more expensive Russian *papirosy* [cigarettes]. Seeing Father's pleasure, she laughed. "What a rewarding Woman's Day party it was!" She looked at us two and said: "Now, let's get ready to hop into our beds. Dawn is not far off. School is waiting!"

Slava and I returned to our still warm beds, pleased beyond words with our presents. One hard candy was in my mouth, lying between cheek and gum, melting slowly. I was in bliss, preparing to fall asleep as soon as the candy completely melted.

After a few minutes at the samovar, our parents, too, went to bed, and sleep's rhythmic, soft breathing was soon the only sound in the house. When there was no more sweet liquid to extract in my mouth, I, too, began to fall asleep.

Then, thunder! Thunder? To my half-sleeping brain the noise of an approaching motor car sounded like roaring thunder. The noise burst into our room, alerting us to danger. No one in all of Dulovo [the city where Malkovna's family lived] owned a car privately. It could only be a "black crow"—a long, official vehicle, the function of which was to carry arrested individuals to the cellars of the NKVD [the Soviet secret police]. It sputtered to a stop, directly outside our house.

> It could only be a 'black crow'—a long, official vehicle, the function of which was to carry arrested individuals to the cellars of the NKVD.

Father leaped out of bed and began to dress. He did not have far to reach. By his side of the bed stood a chair with his warmest clothes. A quilted long jacket, called *tolstovka*—in honor of Count Leo Tolstoy [a famous Russian novelist] who, in his later years, so liked to dress as a peasant—was on the chair together with a pair of quilted, dark gray overalls. A fur hat with ear flaps, mittens, a woolen scarf and socks—all were waiting to be used in emergency. Even in the summer months, when the temperature approached 90 degrees Fahrenheit, those articles remained permanently on the bedside chair, becoming a familiar, even comforting feature in our home. Father's internal passport, cigarettes, reading glasses, and a small bottle of vodka—to calm the nerves—all lay on top of the *tolstovka*. Under the chair stood a pair of very long felt boots and a large sack of *suhary*—dried pieces of bread.

Watching Father dress, Slava and I started to shiver. That chair with Father's clothes, with its felt boots and bundle—it had stood there for more than a year, undisturbed. It was our security blanket of a sort. We were not frightened by this chair when "clothed," since it meant Father was home, safe, with us. But seeing it emptying, exposing its seat and back and legs, we felt as if some ugly skeleton had entered our home.

Fear of Arrest

Mother's face, only a bit earlier laughing, dividing the sweets, became distorted by anguish.

"Darling, darling husband," she began to chant in that peculiar, sing-song way that Russian women often do, when faced with great unhappiness. "I didn't want to worry you earlier. Zikin was at the party. My falcon, my Mark. Try to hold on to your warm clothing. Don't smoke away your rations. Mark, my wedded husband, my one and only. Try to preserve yourself. Try to return to us, Mark, darling. For what? . . . Why? . . ."

Father was dressing quickly, as if he had rehearsed the procedure many times before. His nose became very prominent, thin and pale, and his eyes almost black, severe, yet very sad.

The steps of heavy, official, leather boots, crunching the snow path, were nearing our entrance. We, all four, stood staring at the door, all four separated from one another, as if to touch, to embrace would somehow kill us all.

"Open up! NKVD!" The solid door danced under the barrage of boots and fists. Father reached for Mother and, pressing her to his chest, he repeated over and over, as if convincing himself, "I'll survive, wifie. I'll survive. I won't give in. Streltsy,[1] you know." He tried to smile. "You don't give in either, Natashinka—for the children's sake."

The violent knocks resumed. Father crushed Slava and me in his farewell embrace and, as if in a hurry to get away from us, from the heavy sorrow of parting, he shouted to those outside, "I am ready!"

Unbolting the door, he faced the officials with a bundle in one hand, and the other holding his passport. An out-of-town NKVDist burst into our home with Zikin, the bayanist [a person who plays the bayan, an accordion], who sprang at once toward Father.

He pushed away Father's hand that was holding the passport, which a Soviet citizen had to surrender during an arrest, and barked in a shrill voice, "Go to hell with your f------ passport, you old whore's bastard! A tool! We need a tool! A hammer! We've got car trouble! Can't you move, you son of a much laid mother?"

Father remained standing, uncomprehending, as if he was being addressed in some foreign tongue, rather than the everyday, profanity-filled language of Soviet officialdom.

Zikin, losing patience, swung his huge fist at Father's jaw. "Move, son of a bitch! Hammer!" he roared.

Only then did Father realize that it was not to arrest him, to tear him away from his family, that those people had come. He hurried toward the corner where he kept his tools, and returned with a hammer. The intruders retreated to their limousine without another word.

Zikin, hammer in hand, crawled underneath the car, while from the windowless rear seat, a man's voice trying to shout something was stifled quickly into silence. We four clung to one another at the still wide-open entrance door, not believing that we could close it, bolt it. After what seemed to us endless hammering, grunting, and cursing, we heard the car's motor start to murmur, then with a great roar, the much-dreaded "crow" jumped forward and raced away from our house. Only then the tears came.

The kitchen table welcomed us once more, with its cookies, candies, expensive cigarettes—those rewards that had come Mother's way just a few hours earlier—rewards for being a woman. There in the kitchen, Mother, Slava, and I, all at once noticing Father's legs, began to giggle through the stubborn tears. He could not understand our sudden change of mood, puzzled by our half-crying, half-smiling faces, until Mother pointed to his long, lean legs—clad only in his dark gray underwear! The *tolstovka* jacket covered him to the lower hips, while the felt boots came almost to the knees; in between—just underwear.

"So, you were ready to face godforsaken Kolyma."[2] Mother's lips parted in a slight smile, prompting me to want to break out laughing. Instead, I threw myself at Father's felt boots, and holding on to his bony knees, I cried out in a high voice, unfamiliar even to myself.

"Papa! I don't understand! I don't understand! Papochka, why were those men so brutal? What did you do wrong, Papa? What? Why should you be afraid? I am afraid, too. I don't want to go to sleep."

Father lifted me from the floor. I shivered so that my teeth began to make a clicking noise. Slava, too, could not stop shivering.

> Our town—and every town in the country—swarmed with children who found themselves practically overnight without parental care or love.

"Let us all climb on top of the *pechka* [Russian oven or stove]," Mother proposed, and quickly arranged our beds in a warm, cozy corner, where it seemed neither Zikin nor the NKVD could possibly reach us.

Swarms of Children

Deep, restful sleep did not come to me that night. The thought that the warm, comforting bodies of my parents might disappear and leave Slava and me *besprizhorniks*, frightened me. *Besprizhornik* means, literally, "one without supervision." Our town—and every town in the country—swarmed with children who found themselves practically overnight without parental care or love. In many cases they were not truly orphans; rather, their parents were separated from them by force, and the state expressed not the slightest interest in the welfare of the children of "enemies of the people." The revolution and civil war [of 1917–1923] produced a wave of *besprizhorniks*, as always happens in every country's internal upheavals. But in Russia, since 1921, even after the civil war ended, with the Communists consolidating their power, the homeless, abandoned children continued to fill the ranks of *besprizhorniks*. Those numbers were swelled in 1927, when the clergy and intelligentsia were punished with exile or death for their "anti-government activities." Another wave of *besprizhorniks* resulted from the kulak [wealthy peasants] and peasant persecution, when many parents were "eliminated," leaving behind such a mass of *besprizhorniks* that it could not even be called a tidal wave. An ocean of fatherless, motherless children of all ages left to fend for themselves, covered the Russian soil from one corner to another.

A new campaign, that of 1934–35, wiped out one-quarter of the population of Leningrad, punishing it for the murder of a Party big shot—[Sergey] Kirov. More *besprizhorniks*. And then, a wave of terror swept across the land, a wave that started to swell a year earlier, and had just knocked on our door.

When a man was arrested, his wife was often fired from her job, because she was considered an "undesirable." Family belongings were confiscated, frequently to the last piece of clothing, to the last cooking pot. The family was thrown out of its lodgings and, in the end, the wife, too, disappeared.

Children in such cases had, literally, to live on the streets or, as in Dulovo, run into the forest. To help a *besprizhornik*, to scrub his lice-infested scalp and bathe him, or to boil and mend his rags crawling with vermin, to give him some dried bread, *suhary*, was officially prohibited. No religious or other charitable organizations were allowed, under Soviet rule, to help *besprizhorniks*. These outcasts, although trying at first to remain decent—remembering their family upbringing—in the end had no alternative but to turn to crime.

Children Turn to Crime

I had had a personal encounter only a year earlier with one of the boys who had taken that road. I was walking home from school with a classmate, when a fourteen-year-old *besprizhornik*, Kolka, decided to attack me. When the 1934–35 wave of Kirov reprisals reached our town, his parents, both high school teachers, were arrested on the trumped-up charge of being foreign spies, because they had relatives in Finland. Kolka, for a while, was clandestinely taken care of by many Dulovans who knew his highly esteemed parents and felt terribly sorry for the boy. Then the boy, on his own account, came out of the forest less and less often for food and other help. Instead, he fell in with a gang of much older *besprizhorniks* who were turning to crime.

On that late spring day, Kolka hid behind a thick clump of Persian lilacs in a park near the school I attended, waiting. He chose to attack me despite the fact that my father personally had given Kolka some good felt boots, warm overalls, and an old rabbit fur-lined jacket. He often brought out a bowl of hot cabbage soup and stood by the gate while Kolka gulped it down, guarding the boy from possible arrest by the always snooping militiamen. One day Kolka asked Father for a knife, saying that he needed it to skin rabbits and foxes he was trapping. Father, although reluctant, gave the boy a knife, warning, "Don't use it for bad deeds, Kolka."

Remembering all the good Kolka had found in our house, I was utterly surprised that he would single me out for an attack. But attack he did. Pushing me to the ground, he began to tear off my baggy, thick bloomers, struggling with the tight cotton cord. My classmate ran back toward school, and spotting our 35-year-old mathematics teacher heading home on his bicycle, beseeched him to hurry to my rescue. Kolka, seeing the teacher, stopped struggling with my bloomers, and pulled a knife out of his boot—our knife!—threatening to kill the teacher if he were to come one step closer. The teacher did not doubt that Kolka would do just that, and he raced back to the school to recruit more men.

Kolka, breathing heavily, face distorted by anger, picked up a flat rock the size of his palm, aiming at my face. I instinctively turned my head to the right, trying to protect my nose and mouth from the rock. Kolka then began to hit my exposed left ear, after each blow saying, "That's for your mother! That's for your father!" And again, "That's for your mother! That's for your father!" He chanted as if in a trance. My ears began to ring with a heavy, dull sound. Those booming, penetrating sounds seemed to reach all the way to my stomach. The tree tops, the clouds in the sky above, all started to wave—far to the left, far to the right. I started to drift into unconsciousness. But before that merciful state could overtake me, Kolka's face swam into view, and I could not understand why he was crying. After all, it was I who was being hurt. Kolka was sobbing violently, while repeating his monotonous chant, "For your mother! For your father!"

He fled into the thick forest when more people ran toward us, and vanished.

One other encounter took place with a *besprizhornik* a few months later, when Father was accompanying me to the dispensary 12 kilometers away, at Orehovo-Zuevo, for a weekly treatment of my left ear which was discharging pus and blood since the beating. In order to save time, we went through a thickly wooded area. Walking briskly along the narrow path, we

> Her long, matted hair fell over forehead and cheeks, her eyes huge and dull, skin covered with open sores. She was shivering under her skimpy, soiled rags.

heard the rustle of leaves, and abruptly stopped. Father, expecting to face an animal of some sort, became tense, alert. Instead, a pale, scrawny girl about eight or nine years old crawled from under a layer of thick shrubs and stood there, facing us in silence. Her long, matted hair fell over forehead and cheeks, her eyes huge and dull, skin covered with open sores. She was shivering under her skimpy, soiled rags.

Ignoring me as if I was not present, staring at Father, she lifted her clothing above her naked hips, exposing a bloated belly, and said in a voice devoid of all emotion, "*Dyadenka* [little uncle], if you feed me, you may f--- me."

"They Led You Away at Dawn"

While lying on the warm *pechka* with both parents near me, I could not erase the memory of that girl—the young recruit to the army of *besprizhorniks*. What name had been given her, I wondered. Anya? Luba? Perhaps Katya? Or Nina? Could I be next? And who would help me then, help me to survive? That day, Father said to the girl to wait for us to return with some hot soup and *suhary*, but the girl was afraid we would bring the militia, and asked for money. The five rubles we gave her, how long would it feed her? And that offer of her body, so casual, so matter of fact. How many girls were there in Dulovo's forests, girls like her? How many Kolkas were there, angry, swallowed by despair, who wept for the loss of their own parents while beating and raping the more fortunate ones?

And so I met the coming of dawn, eyes burning from lack of sleep, body heavy, stiff, unresponsive, as though I had spent all those pre-dawn hours toiling at some exhausting physical task. Over breakfast of tea and *suhary* Mother at one point caressed Father's hand with hers and said, "That poem by [Russian poet Anna] Akhmatova. . . . She wrote it for us, it seems." And, almost in a whisper, Mother proceeded to quote one of Russia's most beloved poets:

> They led you away at dawn
> And I followed you, like a mourner
> In their room children cried, curtains drawn
> While the candle went dark in the holy corner.
> Your lips retain the icon's chill
> I cannot forget your death-sweat brow
> As the Streltsy wives,[3] so I, too, will
> Under the Kremlin[4] towers howl.

After breakfast tea, our parents hurried to the factory, while Slava and I stumped listlessly toward school. I silently kept repeating Akhmatova's poem, visualizing mother howling at the Kremlin wall as the Streltsy wives howled two and a half centuries earlier, begging the young Czar Peter to spare the lives of their menfolk. Those men tried physically to remove Peter from the throne; to kill him if need be. But my dear father—the bookkeeper—whom was he threatening? Why must he fear arrest and banishment to Siberia?

The three-story, modern school building met us from afar with a huge red placard on its wall. There was the image of Josef Vissarionovich Stalin, bigger than life, holding a child in his arms, a Burat [a region in south-central Siberia] girl whose name was Mamlakat; a mass of field poppies were in the girl's hands, as bright as Mamlakat's smile, as bright as her laughing eyes. Flowers for the *Vozhd*—the leader. Under their images was printed a direct quotation from Josef Vissarionovich himself:

> But my dear father—the book-keeper—whom was he threatening? Why must he fear arrest?

LIFE HAS BECOME BETTER!
LIFE HAS BECOME MORE JOYOUS!

Notes

1. The Streltsy were a Russian military corps. The statement presumably referred to their courage and fighting prowess.
2. Kolyma is a frigid region in the far northeast of Russia. Many prisoners were sent there.
3. The Streltsy fighting force was involved in rebellions. Peter the Great put down the rebellion and destroyed the Streltsy in 1698.
4. A Kremlin is a fortified complex in Russian cities.

Nikita Khrushchev Decries Stalin and the Purges

Nikita Khrushchev

In the following viewpoint, Stalin's successor discusses the fate of two important Soviet military men, Vasily Gordov and Grigory Kulik. He says that both men served the Soviet army honorably and to the best of their abilities during World War II. However, he says that after the war they had a conversation in which they blamed Stalin for reverses during the war. He says Stalin bugged their conversation, and because they had criticized him, he had them both executed. The author says that this was cruel and unjust. Nikita Khrushchev was an important official during Joseph Stalin's reign and Stalin's successor at the head of the Soviet Union.

SOURCE. Nikita Khrushchev, *Memoirs of Nikita Khrushchev*. University Park: Pennsylvania State University Press, 2004–2007, pp. 409–411. Copyright © 2007 by Pennsylvania State University Press. All rights reserved. Reproduced by permission.

It was reported to me later that in the area to which [Andrey] Yeremenko [a Soviet general during World War II] and I had sent [Major-General Vasily] Gordov some very heavy fighting was going on. When he was wounded, we had hardly any troops left in that sector. One or two tanks came by, and the tank men warned him that we no longer had any troops in the area. He paid no attention and continued to occupy a position on some high ground, together with his adjutant. Then an enemy plane flew over and dropped bombs. Gordov was wounded by a bomb, suffered shell shock, and was rendered helpless. The enemy would unquestionably have seized him, but a wagonload of communications troops happened to come by. They were rolling up telephone wire as they retreated, and they found the general. He was loaded onto the wagon and taken away from the front lines. Gordov was placed in a hospital, and the hospital quickly sent him off to Kuibyshev, where his family was located. In Kuibyshev he received medical treatment and recuperated and later returned to the front, but not to the Stalingrad area. I didn't meet him again until, as I recall, 1944, when it seems to me he commanded the Third Guards Army, reaching the border of Poland with that army. He fought well and successfully to the end of the war. He died after the war, in 1951, as a result of an arbitrary act by [Joseph] Stalin. He was arrested and executed.

Gordov's Character

So that was the unpleasant incident that occurred with Gordov in 1942. The memory of him that remains with me is one of a general with dual, opposing characteristics. I had a high opinion of him because of his tireless energy, quickness to respond and act, and contempt for danger. He carried this literally to the point of irrationality, where he risked his life when it was not required of a commander—he moved around when the bombs and shells were flying. Several times I observed him take off his service cap and walk freely among the bullets. I remember one occasion when he and I were on our way to visit [Mikhail] Shumilov, elements of whose 64th Army and of [Trofim Ivanovich] Tanaschishin's mechanized corps were engaged in battle. Tanaschishin was a very brave man. I saw that Gordov conducted himself in an equally courageous manner in the same difficult situation, and I

> I regret the undeserved end that came to this man who gave his whole life . . . to the homeland and to the Red Army.

regret the undeserved end that came to this man who gave his whole life, all of his knowledge and strength, to the homeland and to the Red Army [the Soviet army.]. He gave everything he had for our victory, but after the battle with our enemy had culminated in our total victory he was arrested and executed on Stalin's order!

So as not to have to return to this question later, I will now tell what became known to me about the reason for his execution. I learned about this from a conversation Stalin had with [head of Soviet secret police Lavrentiy] Beria. Gordov and [Grigory] Kulik came to Moscow. (Kulik had previously been a marshal of the Soviet Union, but during the war he was stripped of his rank and title as marshal, and at that time [in 1950] he was simply a general.) They were on duty somewhere outside Moscow, but, it seems, they had rooms at the Hotel Moskva. They got drunk. (Both of them were inclined to drink excessively. Kulik especially was a heavy drinker. Gordov was also a drinker, but it seems to me he was less addicted.) They had both fallen out of favor with Stalin, and the war was over, and apparently they felt dissatisfied and stirred up. They got drunk and had a conversation about how the war had been conducted and how it ended. Apparently in their discussion they analyzed why our army had retreated at the beginning of the war. In this connection they dragged Stalin over the coals.

From the conversation between Stalin and Beria I remember that Kulik had said: "A fish starts to rot from the head." It was clear that by the "head" he meant Stalin. Of course Stalin couldn't tolerate anyone talking like that, and this conversation became known for a very simple reason. They were under surveillance, and their conversations were being monitored. When they came to Moscow, they were placed in hotel rooms equipped with

Nikita Khrushchev (left) and other Russian military officers discuss strategy during the siege of Stalingrad in 1942. Khrushchev blamed Stalin for reverses during the war. (© **Mondadori** via Getty Images.)

listening devices. Thus their entire conversation immediately became known and was reported to Stalin, who then destroyed these men. I think this was extremely dishonorable on Stalin's part. It seems that Stalin was willing to eavesdrop even on himself, never mind those he no longer trusted.

Honorable Men

They were honorable men, devoted to the Soviet government. I had a different assessment of each of these two men. I had a very poor opinion of Kulik's abilities as a commander, but I had respect for Gordov in that regard. I felt he had excellent qualities as a commander. He proved this in action both at Stalingrad and after Stalingrad, when he commanded armies. Everybody has shortcomings. Despite all of Kulik's shortcomings as a commander, he was an honorable person. He devoted his whole life to the Red Army and served it to the best of his abilities, both mental and physical. Before the war Stalin overestimated him as an artillery expert and placed him in charge of artillery for the entire Red Army. This was wrong. Kulik was not capable of handling this task. Stalin himself bears responsibility for the fact that he assigned this man to a post that he really wasn't up to. But why execute him when the war was already over? That was both cruel and unjust, an abuse of power. Once Stalin had gained complete power, he was able to do whatever he wanted, and he did. He both killed people and pardoned them.

> But why execute him when the war was already over? That was both cruel and unjust, an abuse of power.

The Slánský Trial

George H. Hodos

In the following viewpoint, the author describes his show trial during Stalin's reign. He lived in Hungary at a time when the country was under the control of the Soviet Union, and in 1949 he was arrested. He pled guilty to treason and recited the false confession that had been written for him. He says he was then given eight years in prison, though he had been promised three. George H. Hodos was a Hungarian journalist and editor who later emigrated to Austria and the United States.

I remember only vaguely my trial. The gap in my memory comes, perhaps, from the self-delusive wish I had felt to have it over quickly, an unimportant, formal ritual at the end of which the promise is waiting: six weeks in a villa, and I can see my wife again, tell her not to worry, everything will soon be over. The trial seemed to me the door leading to freedom in the not-so-distant

---

SOURCE. George H. Hodos, "The Slánský Trial: Personal Notes IV: May 16, 1950," *Show Trials: Stalinist Purges in Eastern Europe*. New York: Praeger, 1987, pp. 89–91. Copyright © 1987 by Praeger. All rights reserved. Reproduced by permission.

future; I had to pass through it quickly. Important was only what comes after it.

They escorted us, twelve men and two women, through the prison yard to the court building in Markó Street. In the waiting room, our handcuffs were removed. I looked around. It was similar to a plenary session of the Swiss party group in the old times, and the thought made me laugh. But then I remembered that Szönyi was missing, and the laughter got stuck in my throat. Two other comrades were also missing; one of them, as I found out much later, was for some inscrutable

> We were all accused of high treason and of conspiracy to overthrow the government.

reason not brought to trial but sent to an internment camp; the other one escaped arrest altogether, in gratitude for important services he had rendered in the past for the AVH.

In compensation, two non-Swiss were included. Endre Rosta, the espionage boss of my protocol, was probably attached to the group on my account, but also, perhaps, because he had a Swiss wife. György Aczél, a provincial party secretary, had definitely nothing to do with Switzerland. He had been a childhood friend of Demeter and his wife; as soon as he learned of their arrest, he rushed to Budapest and went to the Central Party building in the Akadémia Street to vouch for the innocence of his friends; he was referred to the AVH headquarters where a colonel listened with great interest to his explanations, rang for the guard, and had him escorted straight down to the cellar.

It was a relief to be among old friends. My new guardian angel and babysitter, Lieutenant Faludi, pulled me to the side. He would now introduce me to my defense counsel; he knows of nothing, he assured me, he has no inkling what a political trial means; he was not even allowed to read my indictment.

"We instructed him to ask you only the question, what extenuating circumstances he should mention to the court. Tell him he should ask for consideration in view of your full confession," he said with a cynical, conspiratorial smile. The middle-aged gentleman he introduced me to (I didn't catch his name) was evidently well coached, but to my surprise, he asked me also, do I have children? He then told me that he might add my three-year-old daughter as a mercy factor. Otherwise, we both held to the script.

Then the defendants were led to the courtroom. The audience consisted of about two dozen civilians, AVH torturers and interrogators, probably one or two Soviet advisors among them, and the uniformed AVH guards with their commander, Major Gyula Princz, chief of the torturing squad. On the platform sat the four people's judges, headed by their chairman Péter Jankó. He read the indictment. We were all accused of high treason and of conspiracy to overthrow the government. Jankó enumerated the long list of our crimes: how we had been recruited in Switzerland by Szönyi in the American espionage, how Field and Dulles helped us come back to Hungary with the instruction to occupy high positions in the party and in the government, how each of us had fulfilled the tasks given by our imperialist masters in the service of the conspiracy led by Rajk.

> Maybe I should not recite docilely the memorized horror story, but retract my confession and tell the court the truth.

I listened, but the words did not really register, even the mention of my name did not shake me from the dazed indifference—retrospectively, I think they might have put a lot of tranquilizers in our breakfast coffee. I looked at my friends sitting in the benches, I tried to find a sign of encouragement in their faces, an ironic smile maybe, to show me that they too know that it is only a theater, politically necessary, but not to be taken seriously. There was no response; all thirteen stared fixedly straight ahead. Is the trial really the next to the last act of the show, followed by an early release, or is it maybe a trap that will swallow us? Maybe I should not recite docilely the memorized horror story, but retract my confession and tell the court the truth. . . .

This late, last flicker of human dignity and rebellion died very soon. The chairman finished the reading of the indictment and called the first defendant, Ferenc Vági, to the platform; the others had to leave the room.

In the meantime, the waiting room had been converted into a coffee shop. Small tables were set up, sandwiches were served, espresso poured in the cups, and sweet desserts passed around, friendly interrogators offered us cigarettes; only the white waiter's apron was missing from the elegant suits of the bustling AVH officers. I was bewildered. What will happen to us, I asked Lieutenant Faludi.

"Don't lose your head, Hodos, I told you what will happen," he said soothingly. "However, I have unpleasant news for you. Your verdict will not be three, but eight years of prison. We have to abide by certain juridical forms to save the credibility of the trial, and with your protocol, you couldn't get a lighter sentence. But don't worry, eight years or three, it is just the same. You will lodge an appeal and the higher court will reduce your sentence to the three years I promised. And also, after the verdict, you will remain under our protection. Do you want a certain friend as a roommate for the first few weeks? Yes? I will see to it that you are put together with G." (One promise he did keep, G. was my first cellmate. The other he kept only partially: I appealed the verdict, but it was increased to ten years.)

He succeeded, in any case, in reassuring me. I was the eleventh to be called, and when the chairman asked if I declared myself guilty, I replied without hesitation, "yes, I am guilty."

"Then tell the court when and how you were recruited into the spy gang of Szönyi."

I recited the memorized text and gave the rehearsed answers to the prearranged questions. The only witness called was my spymaster, Rosta, who corroborated my confession. Everything went smoothly and without a hitch.

> 'I hope you don't take it seriously, it is only a theater.'

After the testimony of the fourteenth defendant, Antonia Drittenbass, the Swiss wife of Dobó, who confessed her crimes in broken Hungarian, the defense counsels came to deliver their plea. One after the other condemned our horrendous misdeeds, but implied that we were only the tools of the arch criminal Szönyi, who already had to pay with his life for the crimes committed; their clients confessed freely to the charges, they deserved the harshest punishment, but the court should show mercy and mete out a just sentence—my counsel did not forget to mention my three-year-old daughter as an extenuating argument.

In his speech, the State Prosecutor Gyula Alapi summarized the horror story. In my stunned apathy, I only marveled the careful, elegant English pronunciation of the name of Noel H. Field, and I took sad note of his derisive remark that such depraved criminals as Hodos don't deserve to raise a family, they would only "poison the souls of innocent little children."

Then the members of the people's court left the room to deliberate on the verdict. It took them a very short time, and when they returned, they read the sentences ordered by the AVH—Ferenc Vági: death; András Kálmán, Iván Földi, Gyõrgy Demeter: life imprisonment; Gyula Kuti and János Dobó: fifteen years; Tamás Ács, Péter Balabán, Gyõrgy Somló: ten years; Endre Rosta, Gyõrgy Aczél, Gyõrgy Hódos: eight years; Antonia Drittenbass: six years; Rosa Demeter: five years of prison.

On my way out of the courtroom, I whispered to Vági: "I hope you don't take it seriously, it is only a theater." He looked at me and shrugged: "We are objects of history." Later, in the prison of Vác, I watched for four weeks the light burning day and night in his death cell. One night it went dark. The sentence had been carried out.

A Young Russian Woman Remembers the Gulag

Tamara Petkevich

In the following viewpoint, a young Russian woman remembers life in the Soviet gulag, or prison camp. Her camp was in the Asian steppes of Eastern Russia. She talks about the difficult work, the oppressive heat—sometimes more than 120 degrees Fahrenheit—the bedbugs and lice. She also discusses the conflicts among prisoners and the dangers of trusting anyone for fear of being betrayed to the secret police. Tamara Petkevich learned acting and performed in the camps; she became a successful professional actress after her release.

I was ordered to the office of the [prison] camp's new technical supervisor. He was an unattractive man but had an intelligent face. People said he used to

SOURCE. Tamara Petkevich, *Memoir of a Gulag Actress*, trans. Yasha Klots and Ross Ufberg. Dekalb: Northern Illinois University Press, 2010, pp. 164–170. Copyright © 2010 by Northern Illinois University Press. All rights reserved. Reproduced by permission.

work as an engineer at a large factory. He told me he had appointed me leader of the field brigade that collected hemp [a plant used for rope and fiber]. The position meant I had to be active and keep the brigade on the move, as well as maintain discipline—all things I knew nothing about, nor wanted to.

Not Asked, Ordered

"I don't think I'm the right person," I protested with fear.

He cut me off: "Here you're not asked, you're ordered."

I couldn't imagine my further life in the camp, not even as far as the next day. And now the camp held me responsible for fulfilling the norm and, what's more, for the daily bread rations of nine women, none of whom had ever done any physical labor.

The brigade "drove" hemp fibers. To earn 600 grams of bread, by the end of the day we had to put 750 kilos of fiber onto the scales, light fiber, which so quickly became weightless in the drying sun.

At the end of my first day as the brigade leader, the scales stopped at 450 kilograms, which equaled a 450 gram bread ration. The foreigners remarked, "That willn't do! We'll have to chit like everyone else."

Cheating like everyone else meant that someone had to take on another duty: to run to the dirty irrigation ditch that flowed about 100 meters away, fetch a bucket of water, dip in a twig broom and sprinkle water on the fibers that came out of the loom until their weight would add up to 750 kilos.

The practice was a novelty, certainly not possible at the factory, and one could only guess how the guard would react. The old guard understood everything at once but kept silent. Different people came to collect the hemp from the factory, but no one ever questioned the document stating it was 750 kilograms. Some of them would even give me a wink, as if to say "Well, that's how it is!"

I was the youngest in the brigade, so it fell on me to run from the truck on which the hemp was loaded to the ditch and back. It was fifty degrees Celsius [120 degrees Fahrenheit]; my legs were giving way, at times darkness would settle in before my eyes. It seemed, one more step and I'd collapse dead. And so it went, day in and day out.

> It seemed, one more step and I'd collapse dead.

Two weeks later, just as we were in the middle of dampening the hemp, the old guard called out to us. I turned around and saw our technical supervisor Portnov galloping on his horse in our direction. It was too late to throw away the bucket and the broom. I was caught red-handed. Portnov pulled up the horse alongside me.

"I could expect this from anyone else, but not from you!" he said without dismounting.

He rode on, but I stood still, nailed to the spot. I would have gladly sunk into the earth from shame, such a familiar burning feeling! I could have begged, "Please understand: it's only to keep ourselves alive!" But wasn't that obvious?

The women were alarmed and puzzled by what would happen next. Downcast, we dragged ourselves back to the camp. After work, all brigade leaders had to attend a meeting to get bread ration authorizations. I walked in, feeling as if I were going to be pilloried. Waiting for the supervisor to accuse me of cheating in front of everyone, I consoled myself only with the fact that at least I would be demoted from the position, which would relieve my soul and ease my life. But without saying a word he signed the bread permit.

What were we supposed to do the next day? Hunger was our Scylla, conscience was my Charybdis,[1] and we were caught in between.

I received the bread for my brigade. The next day we continued to sprinkle the hemp to get at least 500 grams of bread.

At the end of the shift the brigade orderly had to crawl through a narrow slit under the loom and, lying on her back, extract the hemp fibers from the teeth of the machine. In this steel frame one could not move. To switch on the machine while it was being cleaned meant to cripple or kill the person lying underneath.

My turn came to be on duty. I was lying under the machine when I suddenly heard a deafening roar. The loom started; my hand was reeled into the gear. I lost consciousness. When I came to, all was quiet. The women pulled me out. My fingers were badly injured, my right hand bleeding profusely.

Only one women from our brigade could turn on the machine—Yulya Eckert. Her hateful look followed me everywhere. She had been among those frightening parchment shadows that we first saw when we came to the camp. By now, she was the only one of them still alive. She managed to survive and worked in the brigade, but her strength was visibly melting away. Yulya was looking for someone to take revenge on. I was the brigade leader, and though my ribs, too, jutted out from starvation in her eyes I was luckier than she was.

I finally managed to stop the bleeding. I was expecting to hear words of sympathy; instead, Margarita Frantseva approached me and said, "You shouldn't be angry with her, Tamara." I knew that myself. Ours was a shared misery. But still. . . .

Trying to escape stuffiness and hordes of bedbugs, we would often leave the barracks and sleep on the ground. After the incident, Yulya had softened and tried to get closer to me. A couple of days later, when we woke up in the morning, we found Yulya dead. How right were the women who had more pity for her than for me!

No Bread

One day there was no bread delivery to the camp, then two days, then three. Twice a day we were given only a bowl of thin *balanda* [prison soup]. The camp commandant issued an instruction not to send people to work.

We couldn't fall asleep. The barracks doors were wide open. The steppe resonated in the distance. The commandant's voice was heard through the open doors. He was in his office, talking over the phone to the town officials: ". . . Five days and no bread! The camp isn't working! I can't let people starve behind the barbed wire . . . If you don't ship bread tomorrow, I'll open the gates and set them all free, everyone who's still able to stand on their feet! Let them all go wherever they want . . ."

The commandant was young and we hardly ever saw him in the zone. I remembered one night, while inspecting the camp, he called on our barracks with a female graduate of the Medical Institute who worked here as a doctor. The young woman wore a pink dress; he was wearing his uniform. I peered out at them from my corner on the upper bunk. I thought I was dreaming it. They were so young, and it was obvious they were happy together. I blessed them in my mind.

Soon the bread was delivered, and we started to work again, until everything grew dark before our eyes.

We went to work in tattered bras and filthy, faded knickers. The rest of the clothes some of us might still have retained were burnt by the sun. My "sun-dress," which I cut out from the lining of my coat, was living out the rest of its days. The absurd look of our brigade was only made stranger by the French and German speech mixed into our Russian, and by the armed guard accompanying us to work.

On our way back to the zone, completely exhausted, we had to pass through the settlement. The locals stood watching, shaking their heads. Compassionate souls

Photo on following page: Prisoners engage in forced labor at a Soviet prison camp in the 1920s. (© **Popperfoto/ Getty Images.**)

couldn't bear the view and every now and then would throw each of us a cucumber.

Once a private car pulled up by the elm tree behind the camp gates, the only tree in the entire settlement. The women became agitated, trying to guess which of them was about to have a visitor. A ridiculous thought occurred to me: it must be my interrogator!

I looked at the car once again. It was really him. I saw his face behind the windshield. His intent look followed the half-naked brigade passing in front of him, but he recognized no one. I could muster no feelings of anger or hatred toward him.

Every now and then commissions would arrive from the city. Each time we had to line up and answer their questions.

"Any complaints? Bedbugs? Lice?"

We stood in silence. I can't remember anyone ever mentioning that bedbugs and lice swarmed over the barracks and our clothing. Nothing would make any difference.

During one such inspection I heard the voice of a civilian woman from a group of officials standing nearby:

"Which one is Petkevich?"

Strange eyes scrutinized me with undue familiarity. Under her gaze I felt what I really was: neglected, scraggy, infinitely far off from the world to which that woman belonged. I almost thought that maybe someone from the Medical Institute had sent her to find out about me, but it was too far from being true.

Much later I found out that the woman was the director of the medical unit in the camp where Erik worked. She was curious to see me, his wife, whose place she had now taken. But ignorance spared me back then.

One day I was notified that somebody had sent me money. I could hardly believe the news: I had waited in vain for so long. I turned in the direction of the town and thanked Barbara Ionovna for not forsaking me. "I knew you were thinking about me," I whispered into the wind. And then a letter came. Barbara Ionovna asked how I was doing and described how difficult things were for her.

Letters from Erik came sporadically. Sometimes he wrote in torrents, sometimes there would be a long pause. I found bitter explanations for this: when he didn't write, he was fine, and when he did, it was because he felt lonely. He never complained about his life. He had a successful practice as a doctor and shared with me how many prisoners and civilians he had already operated on, including the camp commandant himself.

The Sovkhoz

Bread was delivered irregularly: "It's war!" [World War II] was the only explanation. It became more and more difficult to get up and go to work, hunger and filth made it harder to breathe, the hemp needles constantly stung our bodies. Life was drying up. Had someone asked me what wellspring of life-hope I found to sustain me, I wouldn't have known what to say. But then, despite life's logic, I would remember the moonlit nights of the steppe, the strange feeling of being close to some godly spheres. The steppe and those nights were a temple of sorts. During night shifts we would find ourselves in the heart of the Asiatic landscape.

> At one moment hunger carried you off into unconsciousness; at another it elevated you, and you felt as if you were ascending into the universe.

It was filled with the rustling of sands, grasses, the droning of cicadas. At one moment hunger carried you off into unconsciousness; at another it elevated you, and you felt as if you were ascending into the universe. The earth lovingly beckoned the resonant moonlight down to her, nourishing herself from it, bathing in it, absorbing it. I saw the height of these nights and understood: it's grand and inaccessible, but it exists. After work, falling asleep in the barracks, I dreamed at least once of overcoming the exhaustion, of breaking through slumber and entering the kingdom of these great nights.

Every time I shuffled back to the zone after the day's shift I would sit on the ground, leaning against the barracks wall, and gaze without any thought or feeling through the barbed wire into the steppe expanse. I watched the glaring air vibrate and settle itself for the night. I clearly saw bizarre silhouettes of houses and roofs in the distance. They piled on top of each other, and the sight of a hazy reddish city was thrilling. It was the Fata Morgana [a mirage] of the steppe, an inconceivable mystery.

One evening after work, the technical supervisor came into the barracks. We were all lying motionless on the planks, trying to conserve our last bits of energy.

"Who wants to go work at the *sovkhoz* [a Soviet farm]? They need to build a new vegetable storehouse. They'll feed you."

After a pause, about seven women agreed to go.

"What about you?" he turned to me.

I knew this meant a chance to survive, but it was so hard to force myself to move. I sensed I was personally marked by some sign of life, and overcoming the desire to stay put, I crawled down from the boards.

It was seven o'clock in the evening and the heat had backed down. At the farm they explained that first we had to make the bricks. We dug a pit and kneaded clay. Some fetched water, others dug out the foundation. We worked at our own pace, without any norms to fulfill, no guards watching over us. We could hear children's voices, the peaceful rattle of buckets and milk churns. A woman had just milked her cow and was coming back to her house; a baby started crying; the lights went out in one of the clay huts. Ordinary human life! Was there still such a thing in the world?

The members of the *sovkhoz* were pleased with our work, and it was already dark by the time they invited us to sit down at a table under a canopy in the yard. Each of us received 200 grams of bread. Some people brought salt, watermelons and cucumbers. We had long since forgotten such things.

In the morning there was the usual wake-up call and work in the field. "Will they come and call us again in the evening?"

The collective farm workers got used to us. Each of us now had her own patron who would slip a rotten potato or even a piece of melon into our hands. Once they even treated us to macaroni; completely unbelievable was the invitation to use their *banya* [a bathhouse]. It was ages since we last washed: there was no water in the camp for that purpose. The only thing you could do was to steam your rags and get rid of the vermin for a short while.

Evgenia Karlovna

I knew there were interesting people around me but could find neither the energy nor the desire to talk to them. One person, however, managed to break through my silence. It was our orderly, Evgenia Karlovna, a thrifty and obliging old woman. She didn't go to work but instead kept our barracks tidy as much as was possible without water. Once, while I was at work, she replaced the straw in my pillow with hay so that I would lie more softly. Another day she saved some hot water for me. When I returned from work to the barracks, she would greet me with a joyful cry: "Finally!" Her attention came out of nowhere, for no good reason, and it felt strange to know that someone was waiting for me in the barracks, that someone cared about how much bread I had managed to earn. In the depth of my heart I felt guilty for not being responsive enough.

Betrayal

Evgenia Karlovna told me about her family drama. She worshipped her daughter and loved her husband. "One evening I was sitting at home waiting for my husband to come back from work. I had wrapped his dinner in a blanket to keep it warm. It was already very late when he finally came and stood in the doorway. He locked the door and said: 'Sit down. I have to tell you something. I have syphilis.'" As she was telling me her story, she wept as much as she must have wept back then. I pitied her.

In November a new transport was put together, with my name on the list. I was afraid of the journey, of the new place and the criminals. I wrapped my woolen jacket and shoes in my overcoat without lining and was ready to go when the work distributor approached me and said that the technical supervisor wanted to see me in his office.

> 'You've got to be more careful choosing friends. Do you know what I'm talking about? Someone from the [secret police] was interested in you.'

After the incident with the moistened hemp fibers I only saw him when he sanctioned the bread rations or called us to work in the *sovkhoz*. He had never spoken to me, and of course, I didn't dare speak to him myself.

When I came in, Portnov looked tired and gloomy. He offered me a seat and came straight to the point:

"You're being sent off with the transport because I insisted."

I didn't know what to say.

"You've got to be more careful choosing friends. Do you know what I'm talking about? Someone from the NKVD [Soviet secret police] was interested in you. Your friend Evgenia Karlovna informs him in full detail about everything you've shared with her. Believe me, the best thing for you now is to go somewhere else. I only wish you well. And don't make the same mistakes again!"

The guards outside were already lining up those leaving with the transport. I stood up and thanked Portnov.

"Wait," he said.

He went behind the partition and came back with a pair of woolen socks.

"It's winter. I don't know where you'll wind up. Take these. They're my extra pair. God bless you!"

He came closer, put the socks in my hands and kissed me on the forehead, looking at me with warmth and kindness.

"If only everything could turn out well for you, you dear girl!"

I wept bitterly and painfully, pressing the socks to my breast.

Evgenia Karlovna was among those who came to say good-bye.

Note

1. Scylla and Charybdis are monsters of Greek mythology that posed an inescapable threat to passing ships because of their proximity to each other. In mythological stories, sailors had to chose between confronting a six-headed monster (Scylla) or a massive whirlpool (Charybdis). Being between Scylla and Charybdis means having to choose between difficult or undesirable options.

GLOSSARY

Bolsheviks   A faction of the early Russian Communist party founded by Vladimir Lenin. It came to power in the 1917 Russian Revolution, ultimately becoming the ruling Communist Party of the Soviet Union.

bourgeoisie   In Marxist theory, the bourgeoisie are those who own capital or property that is used to create profit. They are the ruling class of capitalist society.

capitalism   An economic system that includes private ownership of the means of producing goods and the pursuit of profit.

Cheka   The earliest Soviet state security organization, created by Vladimir Lenin in late 1917. On behalf of the Bolshevik Communist Party, it policed labor camps, tortured and executed political opponents, and put down rebellions by peasants. It was the blueprint for the NKVD and later for the KGB.

collectivization of agriculture   The policy of consolidating individual land and peasant farms into larger collective farms run by the Soviet State. It was Stalin's policy from 1928 to 1940.

Communism   An economic and political system that aims for the establishment of a classless society, in which the workers who create goods own the factories and other means of production that create the goods.

Five-Year Plan   A series of nationwide centralized economic plans in the Soviet Union. The first Five-Year Plan began in 1928 under Joseph Stalin and was focused on encouraging industrialization, the creation of heavy industry, and the collectivization of agriculture.

Great Purge (or Great Terror)   A period of terror and repression in the Soviet Union. Sometimes used to refer narrowly to the period during 1936 to 1938 when Stalin destroyed high-level opponents in the Communist Party in Moscow show trials (the Moscow Trials). However, it has also been used to refer to Stalin's policies throughout the 1930s, including his deliberate imposition of famine in the Ukraine and the use of terror against the Soviet population as a whole.

gulag   The Soviet labor camp prison system.

Holodomor   The Ukrainian famine of 1932 to 1933, which was deliberately caused by Stalin.

Kremlin   A kremlin in general is a fortified complex found in Russian cities. The government of Russia is based in the Moscow Kremlin. Thus, the government of Russia, and in the past of the Soviet Union, is often referred to as "the Kremlin."

kulaks   Relatively wealthy peasants or independent farmers. The kulaks were singled out for persecution under Stalin.

Marxism   See Communism.

Mensheviks   A faction of the Russian Communist Party that was defeated by the Bolsheviks.

Moscow Trials   A series of show trials in 1936 to 1938 used by Stalin to eliminate his rivals in the Soviet hierarchy, especially Old Bolsheviks. Confessions were obtained through torture and threats, and executions often followed almost immediately upon conviction.

NEP (New Economic Policy)   An economic policy established by Vladimir Lenin in 1921 that allowed for private ownership of some small businesses while the state continued to run larger industries. It was replaced by the Five-Year Plan in 1928.

NKVD   The Soviet security police force; the successor to the Cheka. The NKVD under Stalin ran the gulag, suppressed resistance, performed political assassinations, and conducted extrajudicial executions.

October Revolution   The conclusion of the Russian Revolution when the Bolshevik Communist party took control of Russia. (Because of calendar changes, this was actually in November, not October.)

Old Bolsheviks   Members of the Bolshevik Party before the October Revolution of 1917. Stalin saw many of the Old Bolsheviks as potential rivals for power and murdered many of them during the Great Purge of 1936 to 1938.

politboro   The executive committee of the Russian Communist Party.

proletariat   In Marxist theory, the working or laboring class.

purges   In a narrow sense, expulsions of members from the Communist Party. More broadly, the elimination by execution and imprisonment of people considered enemies of the state in Stalin's Soviet Union.

Red Army   The army of Communist Russia.

Russian Civil War   A war following the Russian Revolution in 1917 between the Bolshevik Communist Red Army and the anti-Bolshevik White Army. The White Army was aided by foreign forces from Britain, the United States, France, and other nations. The Bolsheviks won in 1921, though some fighting continued until 1923.

Russian Revolution   A series of revolutions throughout 1917 that toppled the Russian tsar and ended with the establishment of a Bolshevik Communist government (the October Revolution).

show trial   Public trials held as punishments and warnings to political enemies. Defendants in show trials have little opportunity to defend themselves, confessions are coerced, and punishments are already determined before the trials are held. Stalin held numerous show trials for political enemies in Russia in the late 1930s. Show trials were also held in many eastern European nations controlled by Stalin during the late 1940s and early 1950s.

Siberia   The vast eastern and central part of Russia, known for its harsh, frigid weather. Siberia was the location of much of the Soviet gulag prison system.

Soviet Union   The Communist state centered in Russia and including many neighboring areas such as Ukraine, Georgia, Kazakhstan, and Belarus. Also known as the Union of Soviet Socialist Republics (USSR), the Soviet Union was founded in 1921 and dissolved in 1991.

tsar   The name for the traditional ruler of Russia. The last tsar was overthrown by the Russian Revolution of 1917.

CHRONOLOGY

1878	December 18: Iosif Vissarionovich Dzhugashvili, who later took the name Joseph Stalin, is born in Gori, Georgia.
1903	Stalin joins the Bolshevik Communist Party, led by Vladimir Lenin.
1914	August: World War I begins. Russia is embroiled. Failures in the war destabilize the government.
1917	March: The beginning of the Russian Revolution; the Russian tsar is overthrown.
	November 7: The Bolsheviks seize power in Russia. (Often called the October Revolution.)
1918–1921	Civil war breaks out in Russia. Leon Trotsky leads the Bolshevik Red Army. The Bolsheviks are eventually victorious.
1922	The Soviet Union, or Union of Soviet Socialist Republics, is officially formed. Vladimir Lenin is its first leader.
1924	Lenin dies. Stalin seizes power and begins public attacks on his rival Leon Trotsky.
1927	Stalin's first Five-Year Plan begins.
	November: Trotsky is exiled.

1929   December: Collectivization of agriculture becomes a major policy focus.

1932–1933   Stalin deliberately induces a massive famine in the Ukraine.

1934   December 1: Sergei Kirov, a prominent Bolshevik leader, is assassinated, possibly on Stalin's orders. Stalin uses the assassination as an excuse to increase terror and repression.

1936   August: The first Moscow show trial is held, and Stalin purges Old Bolsheviks who he believes threaten his power.

1937   June: Stalin begins to purge the army. Top generals are tried and executed.

1939   August 23: Stalin signs a nonaggression pact with Adolph Hitler.

     September: World War II begins.

1940   June 21: Hitler breaks the nonaggression pact and invades the Soviet Union.

1942   August: The Battle of Stalingrad begins.

1943   February: Germans are defeated at the Battle of Stalingrad.

1945   April 30: Hitler commits suicide, and the war in Europe ends. Stalin's Soviet Red Army controls all of Eastern Europe.

1949–1950   At Stalin's behest, purges and show trials of Communist leaders occur throughout Eastern Europe.

1953   January: Stalin accuses many Jewish doctors of plotting against him and the Soviet Union in a so-called "Doctor's Plot."

        March 5: Stalin dies. Nikita Khrushchev takes control of the Soviet Union.

1956   February 25: Khrushchev denounces Stalin's personality cult and his use of terror. This begins a process of rehabilitating the reputations of many who died during Stalin's purges and releasing many of Stalin's prisoners from the gulag.

1991   The Soviet Union collapses.

FOR FURTHER READING

Books

Anne Applebaum, *Gulag: A History*. New York: Doubleday, 2003.

Jonathan Brent and Vladimir Naumov, *Stalin's Last Crime: The Plot Against the Doctors, 1948–1953*. New York: HarperCollins, 2003.

Robert Conquest, *The Great Terror: A Reassessment*. New York: Oxford University Press, 1990.

Miron Dolot, *Execution by Hunger: The Hidden Holocaust*. New York: W.W. Norton & Company, 1985.

Orlando Figes, *The Whisperers: Private Life in Stalin's Russia*. New York: Picador, 2007.

Steve LeVine, *Putin's Labyrinth: Spies, Murder, and the Dark Heart of the New Russia*. New York: Random House, 2009.

Martin McCauley, *Stalin and Stalinism: Revised Third Edition*. Harlow, UK: Pearson Education, 2008.

Norman M. Naimark, *Stalin's Genocides*. Princeton, NJ: Princeton University Press, 2010.

Timothy Snyder, *Bloodlands: Europe Between Hitler and Stalin*. New York: Basic Books, 2010.

William Taubman, *Khrushchev: The Man and His Era*. New York: W.W. Norton & Company, 2003.

Vladislov M. Zubok, *A Failed Empire: The Soviet Union in the Cold War From Stalin to Gorbachev*. Chapel Hill: University of North Carolina Press, 2007.

Periodicals

Anne Applebaum, "The Worst of the Madness," *New York Review of Books*, November 11, 2010. www.nybooks.com.

BBC News, "The Whitewashing of Stalin," November 10, 2008. http://news.bbc.co.uk.

Steve Chapman, "Putin and Stalin," *Reason*, September 5, 2007. http://reason.com.

Stephen F. Cohen, "Stalin's Afterlife," *New Republic*, December 29, 1979. www.tnr.com.

Isaac Deutscher, "The Stalin Pattern for Power," *New Republic*, March 16, 1953. www.tnr.com.

Economist, "Hitler and Stalin: The Q&A: Timothy Snyder, Historian," June 3, 2011. www.economist.com.

Economist, "Kyrgyzstan: Stalin's Harvest," June 17, 2010. www.economist.com.

Gendercide Watch, "Case Study: Stalin's Purges." www.gendercide.org.

Anatoly Karlin, "Translation: The Case of the 'Stalinist' Textbook," *Sublime Oblivion*, May 28, 2009. www.sublimeoblivion.com.

Jesse Marsolais, "Facing Up to Stalin," *Atlantic*, July 2004. www.theatlantic.com.

Simon Sebag Montefiore, "Before the Terror," *Guardian*, May 18, 2007. www.guardian.co.uk.

Samuel Moyn, "Between Hitler and Stalin," *Nation*, December 6, 2010. www.thenation.com.

Christian Neef and Matthias Schepp, "Crisis-Stricken Russians Nostalgic for Stalin," *Spiegel*, May 6, 2010. www.spiegel.de.

New York Times, "Stalin Rose From Czarist Oppression to Transform Russia Into Mighty Socialist State," March 6, 1953. www.nytimes.com.

Arkady Ostrovsky, "Flirting With Stalin," *American Prospect*, September 28, 2008. www.prospectmagazine.co.uk.

Gurdun Persson, "And They All Confessed . . . ," Art-bin.com. http://art-bin.com.

Benjamin Schwarz, "Stalin's Gift," *Atlantic*, May 2007. www.theatlantic.com.

Ilya Somin, "Did Joseph Stalin Commit Genocide?," *Volokh Conspiracy*, November 23, 2010. http://volokh.com.

Spartacus Educational, "The Great Purge." www.spartacus.schoolnet.co.uk.

Time Magazine, "Joseph Stalin: Man of the Year," January 4, 1943.

Websites

Famine—Genocide in Ukraine 1932–1933 (http://faminegenocide.com). This site is devoted to remembering and commemorating the Stalin-imposed Ukrainian famine of 1932 to 1933. It includes memoirs, testimonies, articles, educational materials, lectures, and poetry pertaining to the famine, as well as bibliographies and links.

Gulag: Soviet Forced Labor Camps and the Struggle for Freedom (http://gulaghistory.org/nps/onlineexhibit/museum). This is an online exhibition organized by the Gulag Museum of Perm, Russia and the National Park Service. It includes material about the growth of the gulag and its effects on Russia. It also discusses the dissident groups that opposed Soviet oppression after Stalin's death. The site also includes teacher resources.

Seventeen Moments in Soviet History (www.soviethistory.org). This is an educational site that includes extensive texts, images, maps, and audio and visual materials from the Soviet era (1917–1991). The archive is searchable and includes a wealth of materials on Stalin.

INDEX

Christian Jr./Sr High School
2100 Greenfield Dr.
El Cajon, CA 92019